"As I speak and consult with all types of leaders around the world, I personally encounter these mistakes time and time again. The lessons in *Mistakes Leaders Make* are timeless, and this book should be required reading for every ministry leader. Keep it on your desk and read it at least once a year."

Patrick Lencioni, President, The Table Group; best-selling author, *The Five Dysfunctions of a Team* and *The Advantage*

"Far too often among those with strong theological conviction the idea of 'leadership' is filed under the banner of pragmatism and discarded instead of studied. I am grateful for men like Dave Kraft who hold strong biblical beliefs and still are deeply tapped into the leadership principles that are both biblical and essential for those who have been called to lead and shepherd the people of God as undershepherds. You can make these mistakes yourself or you can learn from those who have made the mistakes and avoid spilling your own blood."

Matt Chandler, Lead Pastor, The Village Church; President, Acts 29 Church Planting Network; author, *The Explicit Gospel*

"Some of our most teachable moments come when we have made a mistake. When we blow it, we are hopefully most vulnerable, most exposed, most humbled, and most teachable. Coach Dave Kraft has devoted his life to helping ministry leaders fully live out their calling and to finish well. Learn from his insights and experiences as you dive into this gem, *Mistakes Leaders Make*. It could provide you with some of the great learning without having to suffer the pain."

Daniel Harkavy, CEO, Building Champions; Founder, Ministry Coaching International; author, *Becoming a Coaching Leader*

"In *Mistakes Leaders Make*, Dave Kraft tackles the difficult problem at the center of many leadership tangles: the unsettling fact that many leaders don't want to admit that they make mistakes, or at least not serious ones. This book addresses some basic mistakes on a basic level. A lot of leadership teams would profit by reading this together."

Douglas Wilson, Senior Minister, Christ Church, Moscow, Idaho

"'Leaders are born, not made' . . . not necessarily. Individuals are placed in leadership and, unfortunately, often learn from their mistakes on-the-job. Some would say that experience is knowing you're making the same mistakes again! Allow me to encourage you to read this book so you don't have to learn every lesson the hard way."

Les Steckel, Veteran NFL Coach; Colonel USMCR (Ret.); President, Fellowship of Christian Athletes

"Dave Kraft's heart and passion definitely come out in this book! It's not just a read for your mind, but also your heart. *Mistakes Leaders Make* is not just for American leaders, but for leaders all over the world. It doesn't matter if you are a leader in New York or a leader in a village in a Third World country; the principles that have been written here span all times and cultures. I strongly recommend that this book should be translated into as many languages as possible so that many global leaders can benefit. All leaders either commit these mistakes or are tempted to. As they say, 'Prevention is better than a cure.' By reading this book, young leaders can be prepared to face these challenges and prevent themselves from falling into these same mistakes. If you lead, no matter how or where, this book is a must read!"

Ajai Livingstone Lall, Founder and CEO; Central India Christian Mission; Damoh, India

"Dave Kraft has given leaders a wonderful checklist of key pitfalls that can sneak up on you and destroy your leadership. Go through each area carefully and evaluate which mistake could be a stumbling block for you. Then follow the action steps that can help you walk forward in the leadership that God has called you to. This is a valuable tool for leaders in churches and ministries."

Dennis Blevins, United States Director, Church Discipleship Ministry (A Ministry of The Navigators), Professional Coach

MISTAKES LEADERS MAKE

OTHER CROSSWAY BOOKS IN THE RE:LIT SERIES

The Explicit Gospel, Matt Chandler with Jared C. Wilson (2012)

Gospel-Centered Discipleship, Jonathan K. Dodson (2012)

Rid of My Disgrace: Hope and Healing for Victims of Sexual Assault, Justin and Lindsey Holcomb (2011)

Redemption: Freed by Jesus from the Idols We Worship and the Wounds We Carry, Mike Wilkerson (2011)

A Meal with Jesus: Discovering Grace, Community, and Mission around the Table, Tim Chester (2011)

Note to Self: The Discipline of Preaching to Yourself, Joe Thorn (2011)

Community: Taking Your Small Group Off Life Support, Brad House (2011)

Disciple: Getting Your Identity from Jesus, Bill Clem (2011)

Church Planter: The Man, the Message, the Mission, Darrin Patrick (2010)

Doctrine: What Christians Should Believe, Mark Driscoll and Gerry Breshears (2010)

Scandalous: The Cross and Resurrection of Jesus, D. A. Carson (2010)

Leaders Who Last, Dave Kraft (2010)

Vintage Church: Timeless Truths and Timely Methods, Mark Driscoll and Gerry Breshears (2009)

Religion Saves: And Nine Other Misconceptions, Mark Driscoll and Gerry Breshears (2009)

Total Church: A Radical Reshaping around Gospel and Community, Tim Chester and Steve Timmis (2008)

Vintage Jesus (trade paperback edition), Mark Driscoll and Gerry Breshears (2008)

Death by Love: Letters from the Cross, Mark Driscoll and Gerry Breshears (2008)

MISTAKES LEADERS MAKE

DAVE KRAFT

CROSSWAY

WHEATON, ILLINOIS

Cover design: Patrick Mahoney and Matt Naylor

First printing 2012

Printed in the United States of America

Trade paperback ISBN: 978-1-4335-3249-8
PDF ISBN: 978-1-4335-3250-4
Mobipocket ISBN: 978-1-4335-3251-1
ePub ISBN: 978-1-4335-3252-8

Library of Congress Cataloging-in-Publication Data

Kraft, Dave, 1939–
    Mistakes leaders make / Dave Kraft.
        p. cm.
    Includes bibliographical references (p.) and index.
    ISBN 978-1-4335-3249-8 (tp)
    1. Christian leadership. 2. Errors. 3. Fallibility. I. Title.
BV652.1.K69   2012
253—dc23   2012007326

Crossway is a publishing ministry of Good News Publishers.

VP	22	21	20	19	18	17	16	15	14	13	12
15	14	13	12	11	10	9	8	7	6	5	4	3	2	1

CONTENTS

$8.99

126471

FOREWORD

As a leader, knowing what *not* to do is often just as important as knowing what to do. Like many leaders, I've discovered a lot of leadership "not to do's" by stepping on the land mines along the way. And like many leaders, I try to share those valuable—and painful—lessons with other leaders in hopes that they'll avoid the same land mines I've stepped on.

I've no doubt that there are future land mines ahead of me. So, I'm particularly grateful to my friend Pastor Dave Kraft for writing *Mistakes Leaders Make*.

I've had the privilege to know Dave for years. He was among a handful of older, wiser, more experienced leaders who came and humbly served me in one of the hardest seasons of my life, when I was tired, burnt out, overextended, and trying to figure out how to lead my church through explosive growth.

It was during this time that Dave personally coached me, helping me find proper balance and giving me wise counsel that saved me from burnout, making me a healthier, more effective leader and benefiting my church in many unseen ways. Much of what he taught me he also wrote in his first book, *Leaders Who Last*. Thanks to Dave's wisdom, many pastors such as myself have learned how to run and finish the race of ministry well.

Now, in his second book, *Mistakes Leaders Make*, Dave once

again offers valuable lessons for pastors and church leaders, sharing this time what *not* to do in order to last in the ministry.

Dave brings over forty-three years of pastoral ministry experience to the table. He's been there and done that. He's stepped on a lot of land mines. And along the way he's learned a lot of lessons. His hope is that you'll learn from his mistakes and the mistakes he's seen other leaders make. It's my hope for you as well.

What I love most about Dave is that he's intensely Christ-centered. His love for Jesus and for those who serve Jesus in the ministry is evident.

Ultimately, at the heart of Dave's list of ministry leadership don'ts is the most important do—keep Jesus at the center. In the ministry, many things draw our attention away from Jesus onto other things. It's in these moments when we're at our weakest, drawn off the path of fruitfulness. This wandering takes shape in many forms, which Dave expertly explores in this book.

Don't just read this book quickly. Rather, process it. Go back to it time and again to continually remind yourself of what not to do, and to examine your life and ministry to make sure you're moving forward reliant on Jesus and producing fruit for his church.

We have a high calling as leaders. The pressure is steep. The criticism is high. And the cost can be high both personally and spiritually. These pressures can cause us to stop focusing on the future and seeing where we're going. That happens to our own detriment. In *Mistakes Leaders Make*, Dave helps us to look out at the horizon, see potential dangers, and make course corrections before it's too late.

For that, we should all be very grateful.

Mark Driscoll

INTRODUCTION

My dad was a locksmith for all the years I knew him. He died when he was fifty-two and I was twenty-four. It was a big loss for me. He collected quotes and had them strung across the counter in his business on a clothesline. One of them I remember well: "Show me a man who never made a mistake, and I'll show you a man who never made anything."

As leaders we all make mistakes—it's part of being human. Some mistakes are innocent and are no big deal. Others are serious and are a big deal. In this book we'll deal with the "big deal" kind.

Some potentially serious mistakes are ones we make only once or twice, and we recognize them, admit to them, deal with them, and then move on. Other serious mistakes are subtler, continue for years, and cause us to derail permanently. They can be compared to a slow leak somewhere in your home that is not discovered for a long time, or termites that have been in the structure of an edifice doing their slow but destructive work for years unnoticed—in due time the damage becomes obvious to everyone. Maybe a mistake has been present in your life for months, even years, slowing eating away, but you have not dealt with it because you've been unaware of it.

As you work your way through *Mistakes Leaders Make*, you might think:

1. He is describing my church, at least in part.

2. I know of a church like this.
3. I have a close friend who is on the staff of a church like this.

My prayer is that in reading this book you will have some *aha!* moments, have your blind eyes opened, and be led by the Holy Spirit to confess, repent, and be forgiven so you can learn before permanent damage is done. I also trust that you will be able to share the ideas in this book with other leaders you know so they can repent and let the truth of the gospel rule, before it is too late!

As leaders, we can have our "sweet spots," situations in which we function well and are fruitful and productive, experiencing God's favor and great joy. We can also have our "blind spots," where the termites are doing their slow but sure work, which causes defeat, discouragement, and derailment, and eventually leads to the knockout blow that sends us down to the canvas for the count, as we see (for example) in the life of King Saul.

Picture King Saul as the lead pastor of a modern-day, Bible-preaching, Jesus-loving, missional church, and you can visualize how most of the mistakes in his life and leadership would have impacted the church he led. King Saul of Israel could very well be the poster child for mistakes leaders make. He made more than his share of them.

A number of years ago I did a personal Bible study in which I compared David's leadership to Saul's. Here are a few of the observations I made based on Saul's actions and decisions recorded in 1 Samuel 13–15:

- Insecurity leads to motivation by fear of failure.
- Circumstances, not God's desires, control Saul's choices.
- Rationalization, not repentance, follows his sin.
- He loses the favor and respect of his son, Jonathan.
- He loses favor with God.
- He assumes the problem is with others, not himself, and he plays the blame game.
- He demonstrates inflexibility and won't admit when he is wrong.
- He seems to prefer popularity rather than obedience.

- He is unduly concerned for his honor and image.
- He refuses to take ownership of his decisions and failings.
- He feels that religious activity can compensate for partial obedience.

Now, King David was by no means perfect and sin free. The big difference was that David owned his sin (Psalms 32 and 51), and Saul did not.

In my first book, *Leaders Who Last,* I dealt with a number of things leaders *should do* to help them finish well, including:

- Drawing on the power of Jesus
- Having a purpose
- Living with passion
- Setting priorities
- Living and ministering at a healthy pace
- Being clear about calling and gifts

In *Mistakes Leaders Make*, the focus is on what *not to do*; this is a strong encouragement to avoid potentially fatal mistakes. We'll look at mistakes that almost ensure that we finish poorly or not at all, mistakes that "disqualify" us from the race that Paul alludes to: "But I discipline my body and keep it under control, lest after preaching to others, *I myself should be disqualified*" (1 Cor. 9:27).

Most of these mistakes you will recognize either from past or present personal experience, or because you have seen them in a leader's life in some ministry context. None of them need permanently trip us up if we recognize them, confess them, and repent of them by calling them what they are: sin, derailers, and booby traps that keep us from being the people and the servants God created us to be.

Sometimes we recognize these mistakes because a faithful spiritual brother or sister, or a spouse, or a close friend points them out. We can receive insight from an article, a book, a sermon, a conference, or a seminar. God can open our eyes as we spend time in Scripture, prayer, and worship.

These moments of insight can occur when we are alone for extended times to be refreshed by the Lord or in the context of relationships—as part of a community group or with an accountability partner with whom we have learned to be gut honest. These times enable us to see the mistakes for what they are, to own them, and to deal ruthlessly with them before significant damage is done. Sometimes we have that *aha!* moment, but sometimes it takes a longer period of time to see the mistakes for what they are.

Throughout this book, I will refer to the experience of Covenant Community Church (CCC). CCC is not a real church but a composite of churches I have worked with in forty-three years of ministry. Although the church is fictitious, the mistakes are not. I have either made these mistakes myself, been in ministries where they have occurred, or coached leaders who have experienced them personally in their ministry assignments.

We will explore how the leaders and ministry teams of CCC experience ten mistakes over the course of five to ten years and how these mistakes affected the lives of many people in the church community.

We will meet:

- Norm, Lead Pastor
- Jim, Executive Pastor
- Jason, Pastor of Discipleship/Community Groups
- Chris, Junior and Senior High Director
- Suzie, Children and Women's Ministry Director
- Bob, Elder who oversees finances
- Bryan, Worship Director
- Brent, Pastor of Counseling/Support Groups

Some of these leaders at CCC learned from their mistakes, dealt with them, and went on to have fruitful ministries. Others were not as fortunate.

One more thing before we jump into the life of CCC. As you read, don't let your first reaction be to take the splinter out of somebody else's eye and overlook the log in your own eye. Search your heart and let Psalm 139:23–24 be your prayer as you move from chapter to chapter:

Search me, O God, and know my heart!
Try me and know my thoughts!
And see if there be any grievous way in me,
and lead me in the way everlasting!

1

ALLOWING MINISTRY TO REPLACE JESUS

Man's nature, so to speak,
is a perpetual factory of idols.—John Calvin

The first and greatest mistake, which in essence gives birth to all the other mistakes, is not allowing Jesus to have his rightful place in our life and ministry. We often start out well with him in the center, but over time the thrill of seeing him at work, the accolades from those we serve, the lasting fruit from our efforts, and the adoration and respect of our peers, mentors, and network of ministry friends gradually become more important than Jesus. Add to this mix our own sinful egos and selfish ambition (James 3:14) and we have a recipe for disaster.

We often don't see this mistake because our experience is like the proverbial frog in a pot of water. If you place a frog in a pot of boiling water, he will jump out. But if you put him in a pot of cool water and then heat up the water gradually, a cold-blooded frog's body will warm up as the water is warmed up, and he will sit quietly until he boils to death. Sin in our lives is often like slowly heating up the water. Our identity in and intimacy with Jesus slowly dissipates, and over time, the ministry begins to occupy center stage in our affections, time, and focus. It is all downhill from there in a leader's life and ministry.

THE STORY

Norm was on the core team that originally planted Community Covenant Church (CCC) ten years ago. He knew from early on in ministry that a lead role was what he was both gifted for and passionate about. He had a vision for reaching the people in Northern California with the gospel that had so radically transformed his own life. It was clear to the sending church that Norm was the one to lead the new fledgling work.

Norm had always possessed a good work ethic (maybe too good), having grown up in a farming community in Kansas. Norm's dad pushed all his kids to work hard from early on. There was not much family time on the farm. Most of life revolved around keeping the farm in good shape and keeping the family afloat financially. Norm's mom made sure they all attended church regularly, and Norm's dad went along with that. But the family was never really close. While in college at Kansas State, Norm ran into a well-known campus organization, and a personal walk with Jesus became a reality for him. Prior to that, he had been a reluctant churchgoer, but he worked hard at everything he undertook and carried the farm ethic everywhere he went.

Seminary brought Norm from Kansas to the West Coast. After earning his MDiv, he served in several large churches before being sent out with a team to plant CCC. The expectations were high, his experience was solid, his love for people was genuine, and his heart was right—at least in the beginning!

Norm had attended some seminars and done some reading about teamwork based on the triperspectival concept of prophet, priest, and king, so the core team was a good blend of all three functions. Norm was the prophet, visionary, and goal setter, with a vision as big as all outdoors. He was complemented by a couple with strong pastoral gifts (priest) as well as another couple that knew how to put feet and hands on a vision (king).

They were off to a good start.

The three-couple launch team had a healthy blend of gifts. By God's grace, they did not make the mistake of having team members that were all gifted in the same way. Norm understood that a team needed to have a good combination of visionaries, caregivers, and implementers.

But as time went on, Norm made several other serious mistakes that were much more harmful not only to himself, but also to the staff and church family. No one imagined that what had started so well could get so bad, especially Norm himself.

The first few years went well. Norm was an engaging communicator as well as a catalytic visionary. Word spread quickly that this was a guy that you just had to hear. Community groups were formed to take care of new Christians and growing Christians who found their way to CCC. The community groups were doing a good job of being missional where they worked, lived, and played; coworkers and neighbors were invited to the groups, to social events, and to worship services. The growth was encouraging and steady.

New hires were added to the team as time went on. Norm's life coach was walking with him and helping him maintain an excellent balance between his ministry and family. Life was good!

Norm was well aware of fallen pastors who let ministry take over their lives (some were seminary friends that he stayed in touch with), and he was adamant that this was not going to happen to him. Godly ambition has an insidious way of morphing into selfish ambition. He didn't have to look far to see young, ambitious-but-proud, and full-of-themselves leaders. Many of them kept close watch on each other's ministry and had a pecking order in their minds as they observed what was happening in each other's ministries.

Despite Norm's awareness of the danger of ministry becoming

the big *E* on the eye chart instead of Jesus himself, and despite the regular warnings from his life coach, the shift slowly and subtly began to take place.

It became evident in staff meetings. The staff felt that Norm was becoming increasingly more driven, more impatient with what was happening, and more dissatisfied with how fast things were happening—or not happening. They were spending less time in prayer and in giving thanks for what Jesus was obviously doing at CCC. They used to spend lots of time celebrating and enjoying each other and what they were called to do. They were truly friends in ministry and often spent time together outside of normal responsibilities. Now the staff felt as if they were business partners with all eyes on the bottom line instead of ministry partners with all eyes on Jesus. The ministry became increasingly about results and less about relationships.

Norm's normal attitude of delight in his staff and what they were doing drifted into demands as he pushed for more and more results and as he became increasingly obsessed with what was happening this year compared with what had happened the previous year. He never seemed satisfied and grateful for what Jesus was doing; he was always demanding more!

Similar things were happening at home. His wife, Jen, and the children began to notice a different demeanor. Norm could not seem to get his mind off of work—what was being done and what was not being done. Date nights with Jen slowing eroded and intimacy dissipated, and in their place came keeping up with e-mails and talking on the phone instead of having adequate time with the family and much-needed replenishing times for himself. Absorption with ministry seemed to drive the joy of the Lord from the family. Jen sensed something was wrong, but she was not quite sure what to do about it.

Norm's affection for Jesus was being replaced by achievement for Jesus, and he just didn't see it or seem willing to own it.

People approached Norm about the mistake he was making, but he was quick to rationalize that everything he was doing was for God's glory, and he insisted that the church needed to grow and reach the community. It was clear to everybody but Norm that he had gone from being led to being driven.

A few more years went by. The staff eventually became tired of confronting Norm. Various pastors and support staff had one-on-one conversations with him, but little changed. It was unfortunate and disheartening, but he was their lead pastor and good things were happening—they could all agree on that. But deep down, most of them were gravely concerned that their ministry was no longer about Jesus but about ministry success, and somewhere Jesus got left behind.

It was sad, everyone agreed, but what could they do? The staff and elders' approach was, "We'll just pray and live with the situation until Norm sees it for what it is." Ministry had become the engine that pulled the train of everything else in his life. He couldn't shut it off or seem to relax and enjoy much of anything anymore. His ministry had become his idol, and he valued ministry results more than Jesus himself.

Norm was giving his life and love to the work of the Lord while he neglected the Lord of the work. This mind-set in the lead pastor tinted everything else in the life of CCC: goals that were set, people that were hired, money that was spent, and treatment of the staff.

Allowing ministry to replace Jesus opened the Pandora's box that contained many other mistakes that over time infected the entire leadership team—with severe implications. The first stone had been cast into the water, and the ripples had begun.

PRINCIPLE AND PRACTICE

Henri Nouwen once said that the main obstacle to loving God is service for God.[1] This is ministry idolatry—not agreeing with Jesus that he has the rightful first place in our affections. Ministry idolatry is becoming increasingly widespread in evangelical Christianity in

America, reaching epidemic proportions. It is showcased at network and denominational gatherings, where the focus and conversation is often not about Jesus but about us and what we are accomplishing and achieving. Leaders discuss the latest poster children for ministry success and their methods so we can all emulate them, buy their books, and attend their "how we did it" seminars and conferences.

"Idolatry creep" sneaks up on you because you can easily and quickly justify it by saying that everything you do is for the Lord, believing your motives are pure. We recognize this in businessmen who work obscene hours while insisting they do it all to benefit the family, when in reality it's all about them.

Leaders must guard against ministry becoming a mistress. A mistress is someone who takes the place that only your wife should occupy. Ministry must never take the place of Jesus himself in your heart and in your values. As 1 John 5:21 says, "Little children, keep yourselves from idols." The New Living Translation says, "Dear children, keep away from anything that might take God's place in your hearts." Our hearts are idol factories, and ministry, for many leaders, is the king of idols.

We can start to rely on ministry instead of Jesus to meet deep needs in our own lives. I am convinced that many people move into leadership roles because of people needing them or because being in control satisfies something missing in their own sense of value or worth. I remember John Maxwell once saying, "If you need people you can lead people." One leader told me that the motivation for "his call" to ministry was the opportunity to resolve the problem of his own insecurities and feel better about himself. The Devil is out to snare Christian leaders, rendering them "ineffective or unfruitful" (2 Pet. 1:8), and if he can't achieve his purposes through obvious sin, he will achieve them by taking something that is admirable and good and turning it on its ear to cause us to stumble.

The apostle Peter, in his insightful chapter to leaders, says, "Be sober-minded; be watchful. Your adversary the devil prowls around like a roaring lion, seeking someone to devour" (1 Pet. 5:8). Our enemy can devour us through ministry by letting the ministry itself replace Jesus in our affections. Unfortunately, we are often quicker to recognize this happening in others than in our own lives.

I began my ministry with the Navigators in 1968 and enjoyed thirty-eight years of ministry with them before retiring in 2005 to come on staff at Mars Hill Church in Seattle. During my first few years with the Navigators, I began my drift into ministry idolatry. I had one of my first wake-up calls (I needed several of these before I could truly see what was going on in my life) in a visit with Tommy Adkins, who was a Nav staffer, friend, and mentor to me.

I had just finished a good visit with Tommy, and we were walking to my car parked in his driveway. Tommy had piercing blue eyes, and I was about to personally experience their piercing quality. When we got to my car, he said he wanted to share something with me. "This can't be good," I thought to myself.

Tommy grabbed a sheet from the notebook he was carrying and laid it on the hood of my VW. He then drew out an illustration that is familiar to all Navigators—the wheel. In the center of the wheel was Jesus.

Tommy focused those blue eyes on me and asked the heart-stopping question, "Dave, what is in the center of your wheel [your life]?" I quickly told him that it was Jesus, to which he replied, "I don't think so."

Tommy asked if he could write what he perceived was the center of "my wheel," to which I answered yes. He then slowly wrote the word "men." In the Navigators, finding and giving yourself to faithful men was the centerpiece of our ministry philosophy. Founder Dawson Trotman, in a classic message he preached, asked, "Men, where is your man? . . . Women, where is your woman? Where is the man or the woman who is living today for Jesus Christ because of your life?"

Having men in the place of where Jesus should be was ministry idolatry—plain and simple and painful to admit. The good had become the idol in my life—not noticed by me but by Tommy. He was absolutely right! As we sing in a classic hymn: "Prone to wander, Lord, I feel it, prone to leave the God I love."[2] Even today this sin is crouching in the dark waiting to devour me. I am not actually leaving the God I love, but rather I am tempted to push him to a marginalized place and put ministry in the center of my life, instead of keeping Christ enthroned there.

It is not my intention to give some kind of formula in dealing with each of the mistakes addressed in this book. There are no "four easy steps to deal with ministry idolatry." But I do want to share some things I am learning about dealing with each of the mistakes leaders make. Let me state again that I have made all these mistakes myself, and I have seen people in ministries, organizations, groups, and churches that I have been associated with make them.

So, how have I dealt with ministry idolatry?

For me the first step is realizing that this is a problem for me. I deeply desire to want to confess and repent when this sin comes to my attention, as opposed to making excuses and rationalizing.

It should grieve my soul that I am allowing something to take the place of Jesus in my heart and affections. Like King David, I want to pray, "Against you, you only, have I sinned" (Ps. 51:4). My primary sin here is against God!

Most every day I make the issue of ministry idolatry a matter of prayer, asking for the power of Jesus through the Holy Spirit to occupy center stage in my life. For me, I find that ministry idolatry is an attitude, a mind-set, as opposed to an action. It begins with the way I look at things, the way I think.

Colossians 3:4 is helpful to me: "When Christ who is your life appears, then you will also appear with him in glory." Jesus is my life—not ministry, success, converts, disciples, developing leaders, being respected by my peers, etc. I need to keep being reminded of this truth. Paul says in Philippians 1:21, "For to me to live is Christ, and to die is gain." For me to live is Christ, not someone else or something else. I have several passages of Scripture memorized (in addition to those just mentioned) on ministry idolatry, including 1 John 5:21 and Revelation 2:4.

The Lord uses these Scriptures to get my attention and point out my sin. This is one reason I want to be consistent in my time in Scripture: to allow him to speak to my sinful heart. We used to say in the Navigators that God's Word will keep you from sin, or sin will keep you from God's Word. Regularly reviewing key verses, meditating on them, and praying over them helps a good deal.

When the Lord makes it clear that I am starting to drift, I want to immediately own it, repent, confess, and ask for his help in agreeing with him that he is central. I want to be especially sensitive to others in my family or on the teams I am a part of when they bring this sin to my attention. One of my life values is to immediately respond to God's revealed truth, whether that truth comes directly to me through Scripture or through the rebuke of a family or team member.

Years ago I attended a pre–Billy Graham meeting in San Diego. The meeting was held at College Avenue Baptist Church, and the speaker was Grady Wilson, an original member of Billy's team. At the end of Grady's talk, he encouraged the listeners to ask questions. One of the questions was, how had Billy stayed humble all those years, experiencing so much success and notoriety?

Grady's reply was golden. He said that when the team first formed, they made a deal with Billy that if God would keep him anointed, they would keep him humble. What a great combination for ministry longevity—God's anointing and the rebuke of faithful friends! Pity the Christian leader with no friends or coworkers who care enough to confront him, especially in the area of ministry idolatry. Norm had these people, but to his ultimate regret, he didn't listen or pay attention to their warnings.

I need people around me who are not afraid to point their prophetic finger in my face (as Nathan did with David) and rebuke me when ministry is pushing Jesus out of the throne room in my heart. I don't want to be guilty of the sin of the church in Ephesus in Revelation 2:4: "But I have this against you, that you have abandoned the love you had at first."

Jesus, I want to love you more than I did when you first saved me, not less. By your Spirit and for your honor, make it clear to me when anything or anybody is taking your place in my heart. Help me not to make excuses, but to be quick to own my sin, confess, and repent. Surround me with people who are bold enough to be Nathans for me on the issue of ministry idolatry.

FOOD FOR THOUGHT

1. Memorize a few key passages on ministry idolatry, such as 1 John 5:21 and Colossians 3:4.
2. Who have you allowed to confront you when they see that you are pushing Jesus to the side and allowing ministry to sit on the throne of your life? Who is your modern-day Nathan?

3. What indicators can you look for to tip you off that you are pushing Jesus off the throne? For example: your thoughts, lack of Sabbath, being more driven than led, how you treat your staff, etc.

4. Do you have a Norm on your team? What might it look like for you to pastor him in seeing the "why" behind the "what" he is doing?

2

ALLOWING COMPARING TO REPLACE CONTENTMENT

The grass always looks greener on the other side of the fence.

In the leadership realm, comparing yourself or your ministry to others is a huge issue. I have been to more leadership meetings than I care to remember. When pastors from the same denomination or leaders from the same organization have their periodic meetings, the "comparing games" begin in earnest. We compare results, size, salaries, cars, houses, responsibilities, fruitfulness, breakthroughs, victories, major achievements, and favorite vacation spots. Sometimes we go around the room and give reports, which just seems to feed the "comparing circus." Other than being harmful, dangerous, and unbiblical, comparing ourselves to others is normal. Normal, that is, for our fallen and prideful old nature, which, I am sorry to report, is in very good health these days among many leaders.

THE STORY

Although Jim had no church background, he was fascinated as a teenager by the stories he heard from his high school friends of the huge difference Jesus had made in their lives. This led him on a spiritual search. His friends invited him to church and Young Life meetings. Jim asked a ton of questions, began reading a Bible given to him by one of his new friends at church, and over a period of four months came to believe the gospel of Jesus Christ: that Jesus had died in his place for his sin, rose from the dead, and would one day return.

It was becoming clear to Jim that being a Christian had everything to do with what Jesus had done for him on the cross and nothing to do with his own morality or good works. One evening while at home, he quietly got down on his knees and prayed, confessing his sin and asking Jesus to be his Savior.

Jim grew quickly as he experienced community, continued to read his Bible, and eagerly began to share his love for Jesus with friends at school. Then he was off to Cal Berkeley and, later, seminary. Right out of seminary he and Esther (friends since their Young Life days) married, and Jim joined the staff at CCC. He first served as youth pastor, and then associate pastor, and lastly as executive pastor, having oversight of the rest of the paid and volunteer staff.

Jim has been the executive pastor at CCC for five years. They have been fruitful years, even though Norm can be a hard guy to work with at times, and hard to please. But generally things have been pretty good. Jim is responsible for seeing that all systems and processes are working well, primarily by shepherding the staff. Norm and Jim are joined at the hip in the day-to-day operations of CCC.

Jim does a little counseling and preaches once in a while when Norm is out of town or on vacation, although it seems that Norm and his family are taking fewer and fewer amounts of time off lately. Jim enjoys his responsibilities and feels like he is seeing Jesus do wonderful things in the lives of the people he works with. He has aspirations of someday being called to be a lead pastor in his denomination. For the most part he has been content to wait for "God's timing." At least, he thought he was content—until recently.

It all started the evening he felt led to share with his wife that he was starting to lose motivation in ministry, but he wasn't sure why. For the last several months he has found it difficult to listen to Norm preach. It has been easier than ever before to be critical. He often finds himself thinking, "I could do better than that. When will I ever be given the chance to be a lead pastor and primary communicator as opposed to just preaching five or six times a year?"

It all came to a head on a Monday morning as he was reading in the book of James during his morning time with Jesus. He was hit hard by the Holy Spirit when he read James 3:14–16:

> But if you have bitter jealousy and selfish ambition in your hearts, do not boast and be false to the truth . . . for where jealousy and selfish ambition exists, there will be disorder and every vile practice.

Over the next several days he did some heavy thinking and introspection in light of this passage and his recent feelings. He had to admit to himself that he was angry, jealous, and frustrated.

Jim began reviewing his past. He came to realize that comparing, competing, and coveting had been a problem (and a temptation) for as long as he could remember. Even back in high school, he got his sense of self-esteem, self-worth, and self-identity by comparing himself with others. How was he looking, how was he doing, how was he viewed by others regarding his grades, his clothes, his athletic prowess, and his popularity with the girls?

In his role as associate pastor, comparing was becoming a big problem for him. Every time he went to district leadership meetings, the issue resurfaced. Most leadership meetings he attended depressed him and sent him into a funk for several days after. Comparing and competing was the soup *du jour*. At times Jim was even asked by old seminary buddies when he was going to lead his own church.

Rather than rejoicing in the blessings of God on other leaders (especially Norm), Jim found himself getting increasingly discouraged and depressed because he perceived he wasn't doing as well as he should be doing and he was not advancing in church leadership. As he reflected on his past as well as more recent experiences, he identified feelings of jealousy, envy, and even anger toward Norm and others on the pastoral team. He was a mess!

In a recent staff meeting, Norm went around the room asking for verbal reports on what was happening in various ministry areas. This had become a regular thing for Norm to do in meetings. This particular meeting was especially difficult for Jim. He was having a hard time rejoicing in what others were experiencing. He was mentally comparing to find out where he was in the food chain of fruitfulness. He was bouncing back and forth between envy and pride as different people shared.

He kept asking himself why it was so hard to be thankful for the fruit and victories others were having. Why did he have to ask himself if he was doing better or worse than somebody else on the team?

He had allowed comparing to replace contentment.

Jim now started to see this as a major problem that, if allowed to continue, would cause significant issues in his personal walk and with his family as well as at CCC. What could he do to recapture the joy in his relationship with Jesus and be content with what God was currently doing through him? Should he confess his sin to Norm and others on the pastoral team? Should he share it with some of the key leaders? Was it that big a deal? He decided that it was, and he acted immediately in response to the Holy Spirit's promptings, and Esther's encouragement.

By God's grace Jim decided to take responsibility for his lack of contentment and for playing the comparison games. He confessed, repented, and shared his insight with most everyone. He is not out of the woods yet, but he is keenly aware of the danger that lurks in his attitude and view of himself and is developing a deeper sense of the sovereignty of God and a greater understanding of the biblical concept of contentment. He is learning anew what it means to trust in God's care and concern for him and in what the Lord is allowing to be accomplished at CCC. He is learning how to wait for God's timing in his ministry.

PRINCIPLE AND PRACTICE

Be content with who you are, where you are, what you are doing, and what God is doing through you.

Jim is grateful that the Holy Spirit (using the Word of God) put his finger on a huge issue in his life, which had been growing for many years but is now being addressed. Leadership mistakes are often not a single event but an attitude, habit, or mind-set that has been forming for years. Now the key to continued victory for Jim is how he deals with his sin going forward in the power of the Holy Spirit.

Many, if not most, leaders have fallen into the trap of comparing and competing with others in ministry as Jim did. It can fuel discord, dissension, and jealousy on staff teams, and it never results in anything pleasing to Jesus. Jealousy and coveting among church staff is often the white elephant in the room. It seldom bears good fruit and can create huge dysfunctions and trust barriers.

Let me clarify that I think comparing is a good idea. What? Aren't I contradicting everything I've said in this chapter? No! I think it is good to compare what is happening through me (and in me) with what could *potentially* happen. It is good to compare where I am in my growth and ministry effectiveness with where it is possible to be, with God's grace.

Where I get into trouble is when I compare with others who have different gifts, callings, capacities, and personalities. I find myself often coming up short. Second Corinthians 10:12 clearly warns us of going down the comparing/competing road:

> Not that we dare to classify or compare ourselves with some
> of those who are commending themselves. But when they

measure themselves by one another and compare themselves with one another, they are without understanding.

Doing some self-analysis with my personal design in mind and wanting to see future growth is at the heart of vision and goal setting. It's healthy to compare me with me but unbiblical to compare me with others.

As I am honest about who I am in light of my sin and as I depend on Christ, I am freed up to grow, achieve, and bear fruit. God has created each of us uniquely. No two snowflakes, voices, or fingerprints are alike. And he has never made another person exactly like you. I love Psalm 139:13–14 on this point: "For you formed my inward parts; you knitted me together in my mother's womb. I praise you, for I am fearfully and wonderfully made." And as author Robert Fulghum writes:

> The statisticians figure that about 60 billion people have been born so far. And as I said, there's no telling how many more there will be, but it looks like a lot. And yet—and here comes the statistic of statistics—with all the possibilities for variation among the sex cells produced by each person's parents, it seems quite certain that each one of the billions of human beings who has ever existed has been distinctly different from every other human being, and that this will continue for the indefinite future. In other words, if you were to line up on one side of the earth every human being who has ever lived or ever will live, and you took a good look at the whole motley crowd, you wouldn't find anybody quite like you."[1]

It is unhealthy to try to be like someone else. I have no desire to be like many of the leaders I read about or know. I want to be, with God's grace, the best Dave Kraft I am capable of being. I am going to be different than everybody else, because God has made me the unique creation that I am. There is nobody else with my combination of gifts, personality, upbringing, capacity, and desires. I am constantly in the process of being delivered from the temptation to be anybody other than me. My daughter, Anna, once saw a bumper stick that read, "Be yourself, everyone else is taken." And Walt Disney allegedly said, "The more you are like yourself, the less you are like anybody else and that's what makes you unique."

Let me give some biblical support for staying clear of the "comparison circus" when it comes to your team, your ministry, and your life. First Corinthians 4:7 says, "For who sees anything different in you? What do you have that you did not receive? If then you received it, why do you boast as if you did not receive it?" The Message paraphrases it as, "Isn't everything you have and everything you are sheer gifts from God? So what's the point of all this comparing and competing?" There isn't any point, if I truly believe that who I am and what I am able to do are sheer gifts.

We read in the Gospel of John:

> Peter turned and saw the disciple whom Jesus loved following them, the one who also had leaned back against him during the supper and had said, "Lord, who is it that is going to betray you?" When Peter saw him, he said to Jesus, "Lord, what about this man?" Jesus said to him, "If it is my will that he remain until I come, what is that to you? You follow me!" (21:20–22)

Here Jesus is dealing with Peter's attempt to compare himself with John regarding their futures. Jesus set Peter straight by saying that what happens with John is none of Peter's business. His business is to focus on his own relationship with Jesus and not size himself up by comparing himself to his good friend.

There is great joy and freedom in happily being who God made me to be: thankful and content with who I am, where I am, and what I'm doing, and not giving in to the temptation of getting my sense of personal identity or self-worth by comparing myself to others. I believe that biblical humility is being content to be simply myself. This is what Romans 12:3 is getting at: "For by the grace given to me I say to everyone among you not to think of himself more highly than he ought to think, but to think with sober judgment, each according to the measure of faith that God has assigned."

Comparing shows that I don't trust the sovereignty of God in my life. It reveals that I don't really accept and am not genuinely thankful for who I am and what God is allowing me to accomplish. It shows that I am jealous and envious of others.

I deal with the temptation to compare myself to others by praying daily, filling my mental hard drive with verses like those above, and confessing my sin as soon as I am aware that I am again headed down the comparison road. I want to nip it in the bud before it starts to dictate and control my behavior. Regularly I ask the Lord to help me be content with *who I am, where I am, what I'm doing,* and *what he is doing.*

Who I am. This has to do with being self-aware: aware of who I am and who I am not. I need to be aware of my strengths and weaknesses. I want to know my capacity and limits, when I have hit the wall emotionally, physically, or relationally. I ask the Lord to show me when I need to step it up and when I need to slow it down.

Where I am. I need God's grace to serve wholeheartedly where I am, not where I would like to be. Paul writes in Philippians 4:11: "Not that I am speaking of being in need, for I have learned in whatever situation I am to be content." Serve God where you are, because you can't serve God where you aren't. This might seem like a simple statement, but it can be profound when we live it out by his grace.

What I'm doing. It is so easy to think that the grass is greener on the other side of the fence. I want to trust the sovereign Lord that he has sovereignly placed me where I am and given me what I am doing. I want to experience his giving me the work to do and the energy to do it.

What God is doing. For me, this is the hardest one to live out. I am ambitious and want to see lots happen. I need to be careful that my noble ambitions for the kingdom of God don't degenerate into ignoble ambitions for my own kingdom. James 3:13–14 speaks to my heart on the ambition issue:

> Who is wise and understanding among you? By his good conduct let him show his works in the meekness of wisdom. But if you have bitter jealousy and selfish ambition in your hearts, do not boast and be false to the truth.

I admit that I hate to wait. But I have learned a lesson from the giant bamboo of Asia. In his book *An Enemy Called Average*, John L. Mason writes:

> During the first four years they water and fertilize the plant with seemingly little or no results. Then the fifth year they again apply water and fertilizer—and in five week's time the tree grows ninety feet in height.
>
> The obvious question is: did the Chinese bamboo tree grow ninety feet in five weeks, or did it grow ninety feet in five years? The answer is, it grew ninety feet in five years. Because if at any time during those five years the people had stopped watering and fertilizing the tree, it would have died.[2]

What a tremendous spiritual lesson that giant bamboo holds for us who are leading and praying for lasting fruit from our labors. Mark 4:26–27 says:

> A farmer planted seeds in a field and then he went on with his other activities. As the days went by [how about four years?], the seeds sprouted and grew without the farmers help. (NLT)

Remembering the illustration of the giant bamboo helps me to have more patience with people in process, more patience for the planted seed (truth, teaching, prayer) to break the surface and be evident. I need to constantly remind myself that God is Lord of the harvest, not me. For me that means he is Lord of the results! Isn't that what harvest is all about—results? The Lord has his timetable.

Nothing is impossible for him. He is at work even when I don't see it; and I often don't see it when I would like to see it.

In summary, I bathe myself in Scripture, memorizing passages and praying them into my life and attitudes. I want to be quick to deal with the ugliness of jealousy, comparing, competing, and not being content with who I am. I want to confess and repent and do so in the context of genuine community.

> Jesus, forgive me for not being content in allowing you to be Lord over all aspects of my life and ministry. I ask for forgiveness for comparing myself with those I view as more gifted and blessed than I am, as well as those whom I deem less gifted and blessed. I can be so selfishly vain and think that life is all about me when it should be all about you. Empower me to trust you and embrace what you have arranged for me. Help me to truly accept at a heart level that you are the sovereign Lord of the harvest, and that you can do as you wish with what belongs to you.

FOOD FOR THOUGHT
1. How would you define contentment?
2. How can contentment, godly ambition, and initiative coexist?
3. What signs would you look for to tip you off that comparing is replacing contentment?
4. What are some benefits of learning how to be content with who you are, where you are, what you are doing, and what God is doing through you?
5. Are you like Jim?
6. Are you teamed with a Jim? How could you point out the comparing and competing and lead this Jim to repentance?

3

ALLOWING PRIDE TO REPLACE HUMILITY

Pride is the greatest enemy and humility
our greatest friend.—John Stott

Pride is a difficult issue for leaders to recognize in themselves and
even more difficult to deal with. It often hides under the cloak of
confidence and conviction. It is the root cause for the undoing and
fall of most leaders. Pride was the underlying reason for the fall of
the angel who became Satan and the principal reason why Adam
and Eve rebelled (so they could be more like God). I find that pride
is often present in younger leaders who are successful early in their
ministry. Proverbs 16:18 clearly states: "Pride goes before destruction and a haughty spirit before a fall." Who in their right mind
would opt for destruction?

THE STORY

Jason is the wild one on the CCC team. He could have just as easily
wound up in prison as on the church staff. He lived to the hilt in his
teen years, giving his family and friends no end of grief. Although
he was raised in a small, Bible-preaching church in West Texas, his
appetite and desire to live on the edge was as big as Texas itself, and

he saw no need for God in his life. He did it all and experienced it all before he was fifteen—drugs, drink, sex, and numerous run-ins with the law. His parents had about given up on him, but they and others at their church continued to pray.

Through some Christian friends at school who kept after Jason and kept loving him, the Holy Spirit opened his eyes. He came to realize the path of destruction he was on and responded to the "hound of heaven," experiencing a profound conversion toward the end of his senior year of high school. The change was so profound that many of his high school drinking and partying buddies couldn't believe what happened to him. His break from old habits and friends was complete. He soaked himself in Scripture and entered a humble and dependent walk with the Lord.

After his family relocated to the West Coast, he found his way into the post-high group at CCC. Although he was clean and sober and determined to stay that way, he was still very immature and had that Texas strut about him. In spite of this, many of the leaders at CCC saw some real potential in him. His outgoing and risk-taking demeanor attracted many of the junior high and high school students.

Without even trying, Jason was the pied piper for the younger set. His name came up from time to time in staff meetings as well as among some of the parents concerning whether Jason should be invited to assume a formal role at CCC. Some were against it due to his sordid background and lack of theological training. He had no college degree or formal Bible training. He clearly had leadership potential, but was he grounded enough theologically and mature enough spiritually? He was smart, winsome, adventuresome, and as outgoing as they come, but was he ready for serious responsibility?

It certainly didn't hurt that Jason had Hollywood good looks and was very athletic, having lettered in three sports in his high school. He was bold, confident, and winsome, but still young as a Christian and for a major leadership role. Some people had serious concerns.

Norm was always on the lookout for young leadership and took a liking to Jason almost from the day he first showed up at a worship service. Everything about him caused a buzz in Norm's spirit. This was just the kind of young man that he needed to get the youth ministry cooking with new life.

Norm had dreams about the youth ministry busting out the doors, and maybe Jason was the key to that. It took a while to convince the staff, but finally Norm offered Jason the role of junior and senior high director. To satisfy some of the staff members' concerns, Norm agreed to be Jason's coach and to walk with him. It was both a way to help Jason and to protect him from the more traditional-thinking leaders on his staff.

Jason was full of initiative and ideas. He moved quickly, thought quickly, decided quickly . . . as a matter of fact, he did everything quickly. Norm loved it. The youth ministry mushroomed overnight. Jason had an idea a minute and created a sense of excitement that caught everyone's attention, even his detractors.

One thing, however, soon became apparent to everyone, friend and foe. Jason was good at doing, but not equally good at delegating. He was the fire and force behind almost everything. So although the youth ministry grew quickly, it was significantly disorganized and lacked depth. What no one could clearly see in the beginning was what was driving Jason. What Norm and a few others saw as confidence and boldness really was a heart full of pride that knew no bounds and was gaining steam by the day.

When Jason had turned to the Lord four years prior, it had been a true and deep conversion; he was truly repentant and humble. But due to early successes at CCC and fawning followers among the youth, along with the praise Norm gave him, the youth ministry soon became all about Jason. Norm probably did see the pride begin to surface, but decided not to call it out, as he really liked what was happening and didn't want to put a damper on it in any way. Norm, in subtle ways, actually encouraged and fed Jason's pride.

Jason's sin of pride grew over time. Instead of his successes leading to gratitude and deepening humility before the Lord, it led to a sort of bullying his way through ministry, becoming overly opinionated, not being open to the ideas of others, and especially not being willing to listen to the concerns of his elders. Somehow he missed the part in 1 Peter 5 about "you who are younger, be subject to the elders" (v. 5).

He was becoming a totally different kind of leader, and what he was becoming was not good. Jason's natural confidence became pride in who he was and the responsibility he carried. He began to constantly look for more and more attention and opportunities to satisfy his developing ego. He had to win and be the best at everything he undertook. He loved the numerical reports on what was happening in the youth ministry; he even embellished the truth at times. He loved being first, best, fastest, and always right. He relished all the accolades he got from parents as well as the youth themselves.

Rather than confronting Jason, Norm tried to convince most of the staff that everything was okay and that these things were just part of being a young visionary leader. So instead of Norm (or anyone else) dealing with Jason's prideful heart, they actually (believe it or not) rewarded him by putting him in charge of the discipleship and small groups and bringing him onto the pastoral staff. To his credit, Jason did then take some online courses in theology to be better equipped with sound doctrine.

Elder Bob had the most problems with Jason, not because of the obvious pride issues, but because of Jason's inattention to detail and not getting paperwork to Bob in a timely fashion. For Bob, how things were done was just as important as whether they were done. Because of his high-flying and fast-moving personality type, paperwork was the last thing on Jason's priority list, when he bothered to create a priority list at all.

The bottom line was that Norm was willing to overlook the

character issues because of the quick results Jason produced in the youth ministry and undoubtedly would bring to discipleship and small groups. The staff could find others to build the depth, but they looked to Jason to get things moving, and moving quickly. This was extremely important to Norm and his desire (wrongly motivated) to grow quickly.

Several concerned older men in the church tried to share with Jason what they had observed, but he would not listen, writing off their concerns as jealousy and not understanding his youthful passion, gifting, and great ideas for making things happen. It was sad to see a once humble, grateful young man quickly become a proud, unteachable leader who was using the ministry as a platform to build his own reputation and kingdom. He was also getting opportunities to speak at youth camps and conferences up and down the West Coast; too much success too early was not helpful. At an informal breakfast with some older and wiser leaders at CCC, they lamented that they knew many young leaders like Jason—arrogant, proud, and unteachable. Where were the young, gifted, anointed, but humble leaders for the next generation?

Jason eventually received an offer from a megachurch in Southern California, handed in his resignation, and left CCC. This was yet another example of competence trumping character. So often it seems we hire people based on their competence (what they can do) and wind up letting them go based on their character (what they have become). The megachurch church didn't do its homework or talk with anybody at CCC. Jason lasted a few years there, and due to moral failure, was later let go. The last thing we heard about Jason was that he was living with a woman and making tons of money at a start-up company. Oh what could have been!

PRINCIPLE AND PRACTICE

Scripture has a lot to say about pride and its destructive consequences as well as the value of humility.

> I dwell in the high and holy place,
>   and also with him who is of a contrite and lowly spirit,
> to revive the spirit of the lowly,
>   and to revive the heart of the contrite. (Isa. 57:15)

> The greatest among you shall be your servant. Whoever exalts himself will be humbled, and whoever humbles himself will be exalted. (Matt. 23:11–12)

In his book *Thirsting for God,* Gary Thomas has several chapters devoted to the topic of humility, and in those chapters he quotes some of the early church fathers. Here is one that really helped me:

> All the saints are convinced that sincere humility is the foundation of all virtues. This is because humility is the daughter of pure charity, and humility is nothing else but truth. There are only two truths in the world, that God is all, and the creature is nothing.[1]

And this is from Gary himself: "Proud women and men relate everything back to themselves. They are all but incapable of seeing any situation except for how it affects them. Empathy is something they may read about but will never truly experience."[2] That described Jason to a T.

One would think that the last thing any Christian leader would want is to fall from a loving and vibrant relationship with Jesus or from being usable by Jesus.

For years I've been acquainted with the concept of humility as clearly taught in God's Word. In my definition of a leader in *Leaders Who Last,* I include humility as foundational to being a leader who lasts. But recently I have begun to gain a deeper and slightly different understanding of what true biblical humility actually is.

A humble person is so centered in Jesus, so much at peace and at home in Christ and his love and acceptance, that neither people nor circumstances take him on a roller coaster ride. You and I will never achieve this perfectly because we are all sinful and in need of rescue by the Savior, but this is what we are moving toward, by God's grace.

I used to think that humility meant staying in the background, not saying much, being embarrassed when I was complimented, and regularly reminding myself that I was nothing. I now realize that true humility is a strong sense of God-confidence, which interesting enough can often be confused with pride and self-confidence. True humility should lead to a strong confidence in how God made me and to honestly living that out, not in a prideful way but in a grateful and honest way. Humility is being yourself, the person that God created you to be, and being thankful for who you are. Humility is not trying to be less or more than you are, but having sober judgment (Rom. 12:3) as to who you are, and who you aren't. C. J. Mahaney writes, "Humility is honestly assessing ourselves in light of God's holiness and our sinfulness."[3]

Luke 14:11 says, "He who humbles himself will be exalted." In The Message it reads, "If you're content to be simply yourself, you will become more than yourself." As I have meditated on this verse, I have come to understand that true humility is being myself—no more and no less. Humility is having an appropriate and accurate estimate of myself. It is not a matter of thinking less about myself (as I have been taught), but about accepting who God made me to be (see Psalm 139). And Romans 12:3 warns us not to think of ourselves more highly than we should or, as the New Living Translation has it: "Be honest in your evaluation of yourselves."

I am beginning to understand that humility requires my getting a handle on who I am and then accepting and being content with that—not wishing I were somebody else, which is easy and tempting to do. I am tempted to think, "If only I were somebody else or someplace else, I would be more effective. If I only had so-and-so's gifts and personality, my life and ministry would be better."

Both my salvation and my calling to colabor with God is all his idea; they are gifts prepared for me and made clear to me. I had absolutely nothing to do with them. My calling and ministry is a reflection of God's design of me. Why then would I choose to be somebody else? I can make two mistakes in this area. I can be envious of someone else and want to be like him or her, and I can be prideful in thinking that others should be like me. Pride and envy are close cousins. Pride is thinking so highly of myself that I wish people were more like me. Envy is wishing I were like other people. It is not a matter of thinking more of myself or less of myself, but thinking more of Jesus. The more I dwell on the cross, the gospel, the resurrection, and the incredible grace that has been offered to me, the less I focus on me.

I find that extended time spent in serious meditation of scriptural truth changes the way I view things—especially myself! Recall that when we looked at the mistake of comparing ourselves to others, we considered 1 Corinthians 4:7: "For who sees anything different in you? What do you have that you did not receive? If then you received it, why do you boast as if you did not receive it? I return to this verse more than any other. "Dave," I say to myself, "if you really, truly believe that everything you have and are (gifts, personality, experiences, upbringing, education, capacity, limitations, intelligence, opportunities, blessing, and fruit) are sheer gifts (as The Message paraphrases it), why do you need to become prideful, compare and compete, or be envious of others?"

Little by little, with God's grace, I am learning to accept and rejoice in how he made me and am being delivered from comparing and competing, choosing, rather, to be humble before him. My new understanding of humility is leading to more enjoyment in my leadership responsibilities. It is limiting the fear and inhibitions I had lived with for years.

I clearly remember the first time I became aware of how deeply rooted pride was in my life. I had been a Christian for about four years, when I was selected to move into a training home with the Navigators in the Los Angeles area. That in itself led to a degree of pride. I was delivering mail for the US Post Office at the time. On my route was a married couple with two small boys. Brian was six and Steve was four. One night they invited me to dinner (single guys take every opportunity to get a home-cooked meal) at their home. Because both boys were memorizing Bible verses before they could read, I asked Brian to quote me his latest verse. In his boyish, squeaky voice he recited Psalm 115:1: "Not to us, O LORD, not to us, but to your name give glory, for the sake of your steadfast love and your faithfulness!" The Lord leveled me as soon as I heard that verse. I went home after dinner, got down on my knees, and confessed my pride, arrogance, and self-centeredness. From that day to this, that verse has been a constant reminder to me that it is all about Christ, not about me. My focus should be on what he is doing, not about what I think I am doing.

It seems to me that the reason leaders, especially young, gifted, and early-on successful leaders, do not repent of pride more often is because many are willing to overlook pride and self-centeredness in themselves and others as long as results are being achieved. When a young leader is full of confidence, experiences success early in the ministry, and has praise lavished on him from seasoned leaders—and there is no one willing to be a Nathan in his life—you have a recipe for a future fall.

In many groups and churches, results trump character and relationships as a high value. I question whether there can be the touch and anointing of the Holy Spirit on a life that is full of the self. I wonder whether deeply rooted pride is at the core of most other sin that leaders fall into, such as sexual, financial, and relational sins.

I have seen leaders publically admit to pride but never address it or truly repent of it. Often their followers are so enamored by the success being achieved that they are willing to ignore the pride, in spite of God's clear denunciation of it in his leaders and despite the damage it causes. The proud leader who is full of himself cannot lead people in a biblical manner, and he will sooner or later manipulate and intimidate his way to success, using people as a means toward and springboard for his ungodly desires.

If you were to ask Christian leaders what the key New Testament passages on leadership were, many, if not most, would say 1 Timothy 3 and Titus 1. Some, but probably not many, would reference 1 Peter 5. Right in the middle of that chapter is verse 5: "Likewise, you who are younger, be subject to the elders. Clothe yourselves, all of you, with humility toward one another, for *God opposes the proud but gives grace to the humble.*"

Leader, if you are a Jason-in-the-making, heed Peter's words: God will oppose you! Confess your pride, repent of it, and make your life all about him. If you have a Jason on your team, consider how Jesus might use you to humbly speak into his or her life.

> Jesus, forgive me for eclipsing you and making what is clearly your work and your story about me. I confess and repent that I am full of pride and self-importance. I am sorry for using people to achieve my ends instead of loving them to achieve your ends.

FOOD FOR THOUGHT

1. Dare to ask those close to you if they see genuine humility or pride in your life.
2. In what ways can God-confidence be misinterpreted as pride?
3. Why do you think God is opposed to the proud (1 Pet. 5:5)?
4. Do you have a Jason on your team? How can you help him see his pride in a way that might lead to repentance?

4

ALLOWING PLEASING PEOPLE TO REPLACE PLEASING GOD

My goal is to please one person each day,
and today is not your day.

Fear of God is the beginning of wisdom, and fear of man is the end of fear of God. You can't serve both God and man. Proverbs 29:25 states it well: "The fear of man lays a snare." In ministry we will always have those who try to push, manipulate, and even bribe the leader into doing what keeps various people happy. The key is to live for an audience of one—God. But the temptation to keep people happy is always nipping at our heels. Many years ago, I read that Bill Cosby said, "I don't know what the secret to success is, but I know what the secret to failure is and that's trying to keep everybody happy."

THE STORY

Chris is the newest addition to the staff team at CCC. He took over Jason's role of junior and senior high director when Jason took responsibility for discipleship and community groups.

Chris grew up in the church with his parents and three siblings and has been in Sunday school from day one, as well as every other program the church has offered. He prayed with his father at a young age to respond to the gracious invitation to have Jesus as Lord and Savior of his life. Though he was young, it was clear to his parents that Chris understood the gospel and that there was no need to wait until he was older for him to be baptized and begin taking communion.

He exemplified what every parent at CCC wanted their kids to be like. Even as a high school student, he had shown leadership ability and was asked to work at summer camps for younger kids. Unlike many church kids (some of whom he grew up with), Chris didn't rebel when he hit the teen years, and now at age twenty-two he finds himself leading the junior and senior high ministry right after finishing Bible school. It all happened so quickly; it almost takes Chris's breath away. To him, it seems like just yesterday when he was attending high school events himself, and now he is planning and leading them.

Even though he served under Jason for a while, Chris was young and inexperienced; he felt like he was in over his head. Jason had been a whirlwind of activity, and he had not spent enough time with Chris to get him ready for a leadership role. But with strong encouragement from important family members and other adults he trusted, he quickly took on rather major responsibilities.

Under Jason's leadership the junior and senior high groups had grown quickly and, in Norm's eyes, successfully. Many people felt that Chris's more low-key and thoughtful personality was just what the youth ministry needed to grow deeper.

Ever since he accepted the role, Chris has been riding a fine line between being innovative and doing things differently than Jason, while at the same time trying not to offend the older generation, which wants a vibrant youth ministry but doesn't want it *too* vibrant—especially when it comes to music and off-campus youth nights. Chris is finding his task to be a lot harder than he had imagined it would be. Part of the difficulty is that he finds himself with different bosses:

1. Pastor Jim, to whom he reports;
2. The kids he loves and leads, who want things a certain way;
3. The parents who have entrusted their kids to him and have certain expectations;
4. The elder board who looks closely at every quarterly report he submits, especially Bob the head elder;
5. Jason, for whom he has great respect and occasionally seeks advice.

No one has actually told him that he needs to keep all five bosses happy, but he assumes that is the case. At the young age of twenty-two, Jason already feels the stress and the pressure to perform and meet everyone's expectations. He wants to do things differently than Jason, but also wants the youth groups to go deeper and broader at the same time. He wonders whether he can keep both quality and quantity high enough to keep everybody happy, or has he been doomed from the start?

He needs to make sure the kids are excited so their parents won't pull up stakes and look for another church. He needs to make sure the influencers among his youth are pleased, as they will have an impact on how other kids perceive the value of what he and the adult team are doing. He needs to make sure the numbers are on the increase so that Jim and the elders know he is doing things right. If he continues building an exciting youth program, kids will show up in increasing numbers . . . right? And if he doesn't? Well, they might just start looking for his replacement. Why did it have to be so hard? Ministry used to be a joy, now it was a job—and a hard one at that.

Over time Chris's situation started to come unraveled. The "five bosses" were sending him conflicting messages. He felt like he was back on his high school football team, but with five quarterbacks all calling different plays at the same time. At times he wasn't sure who he should be listening to, and everyone had a slightly different idea on how things should be done and what results he should be getting.

Since Norm's gradual slide into the "everything being about ministry results" mentality, there was this unwritten rule that every effort had to be a home run, and there was zero tolerance for mistakes or not doing everything excellently . . . dare he say perfectly? As Chris considered the situation, it seemed that things were very different at CCC from when he was in high school. Something didn't feel right, but he couldn't put his finger on it. And he was not exactly sure how to voice his concerns and to whom. The pace of ministry had become faster, the demands higher, and the atmosphere more businesslike and less relational.

Should he mention his fears and questions to Jim? Was Jim part of the problem? He vaguely remembered Jim sharing at a staff meeting that he was guilty of comparing himself with other pastors. Would Jim understand his dilemma? Chris knew in his heart of hearts that he was living and ministering before an audience of one—Jesus himself—but in reality it was hard to distinguish the voice of Jesus from all the other voices shouting at him inside his head.

At times Chris was moved to tears when he spent time alone with the Lord because he was so confused and conflicted. Instead of asking himself what Jesus would have him and his team do, he was asking himself what everyone else wanted him to do.

One day it became very clear to him that he couldn't continue to live and lead the youth ministry as he had been doing. He needed to "man up" and deal with his fears and frustrations. He initiated a talk with Jim and got some good counsel. Jim even shared with him how he had struggled with the same issue of wanting to please people more than God, and how he occasionally still does.

With Jim's encouragement, Chris set up appointments with a number of his student leaders, talked with some of the influencers among the parents, and even got up the courage to talk with Bob.

This was the hardest conversation of all, because Bob tended to be all business and always had his eye on the bottom line—if not the dollar line, the attendance line.

It was a difficult three weeks over which all of these conversations took place. Several times Chris became discouraged and thought of not only leaving his role, but leaving CCC altogether. He began to think that this was not what he had signed up for. One evening Chris's dad encouraged him to stay the course. His father had spoken with several other youth leaders and learned that Chris's dilemma was not unusual. (Maybe that's why youth director positions seem to have such a high turnover.)

Chris became bolder and began to speak with deeper convictions about the direction he thought the youth ministry needed to go. He even mustered up the courage to tell a few parents and key student leaders that several of their suggestions were not going to be followed, and to his surprise they were okay with that. They were satisfied that Chris was at least willing to listen well and take their suggestions seriously. He began to think that most of his fears about keeping key people happy were, in reality, fears he had conjured up in his own head. That freed Chris up to look more at his own motives, convictions, calling, and vision for ministry, all of which he had put aside in his attempt to do what he felt others wanted him to do.

The battle was certainly not over, but he felt that Jesus had given him a new lease on ministry. He was to have many years of fruitful ministry at CCC and would later plant a church in the Los Angeles area. Wow, what a different story this would have been had he quit and not dealt with his fears about people! It would be great if all the staff at CCC had an ending like Chris's, but unfortunately that was not to be the case.

PRINCIPLE AND PRACTICE

After we moved to Seattle in 2001, I went to the post office to mail some boxes. The clerk had a sign next to his window that said, "I make it the habit of my life to please one person every day, and today is not your day. Furthermore tomorrow is not looking good either." Making it the habit of your life to please people is a losing proposition.

Jesus taught that we cannot serve two masters (Matt. 6:24). You cannot serve God and money, or God and anything else that battles for first place in your time and affections. There is room for only one person when it comes to whom you really serve.

Solomon warns us that "the fear of man lays a snare, but whoever trusts in the LORD is safe" (Prov. 29:25). You are in trouble when your main motivator is, "But what will others think if I do thus and so?"

Fear of man and fear of God cannot coexist. Fear of man will push fear of God to the side, or fear of God will push fear of man to the side. You cannot successfully live in both worlds at the same time. But it is a lot easier said than done. It easy to understand but hard to apply consistently in the real ministry world. It takes real courage to stand up for what you believe when you know there might be a price to pay in emotional support, financial giving, or weekly attendance, not to mention potential splits. Jesus said in the Sermon on the Mount, "Woe to you, when all people speak well of you, for so their fathers did to the false prophets" (Luke 6:26). Now that might get my attention. The Message paraphrases this verse as, "There's trouble ahead when you live only for the approval of others, saying what flatters them, doing what indulges them. Popularity contests are not truth contests—look how many scoundrel preachers were approved by your ancestors! Your task is to be true, not popular." Jesus wants us to be true to the Lord, true to our convictions, and true to our consciences. And Paul writes, "For am I now seeking the approval of man, or of God? Or am I trying to please man? If I were still trying to please man, I would not be a servant of Christ" (Gal. 1:10).

I was part of a church a number of years ago in which a well-to-do member decided he didn't like the direction things were going on a number of fronts, and he made some rather serious threats. The lead pastor refused to give in to this member's demands, sticking by his convictions and refusing to back down. The pastor listened well and held a meeting where everyone had the opportunity to express their thoughts and feelings, but at the end of the day, despite the emotions of those who opposed him, he took a firm stand for what he believed was the direction that he and his staff needed to lead the church.

He paid a price in attendance and financial support, but I know him well enough to know that he would make the same decision again, without hesitation. He can still lay his head on the pillow at night knowing he did the right thing before the Lord. There was no way he could keep everybody happy and do what Jesus was asking him to do at the same time. Biblical conviction rather than fearful compromise won the day.

I can't think of a single leader I have worked with or a ministry situation I have been involved with where pleasing people (keeping them happy) was not an issue or temptation. Most of us deep down want to be liked, appreciated, and respected. When being disliked, unappreciated, and disrespected is at stake, it is very tempting to compromise our convictions to keep people on good terms with us, and thereby violate our consciences. We all need to pray for the kind of boldness that Peter and John displayed in Acts 4:19–20: "But Peter and John answered them [the rulers, elders, and scribes, along with the entire high priestly family], 'Whether it is right in the sight of God to listen to you rather than to God, you must judge, for we cannot but speak of what we have seen and heard.'"

I believe that we must take the time to hear from God and ask him for courage to follow what he says. If we spent as much time listening to the voice of God as we do listening to the voices of men, we would be more courageous. I have a section of books on my bookshelves that I most often recommend to other leaders. One of these books is *The Courageous Follower*.[1]

The subtitle, *Standing Up to and for Our Leaders,* says it all. Whatever idea, suggestion, demand, or recommendation comes to the leaders in an organization—whether from above, below, or from a peer—leaders and followers need great wisdom to know when to oppose the idea and when to embrace it. Author Ira Chaleff writes: "In a true relationship, we are neither retiring nor fawning nor manipulative. We work together with mutual respect and honesty to achieve our common purpose."[2]

Over my forty-three years in vocational Christian ministry, I have worked on many teams, with many kinds of leaders, and in fifteen different churches and organizations. I have come to the conclusion that we need to build organizations where there is a culture of candor and not a culture of fear. We need a culture where there is freedom to disagree with others, particularly leaders, to have various points of few, and to be able to express them without fear of reprisal and retribution. No one ought to feel as if he were walking on eggshells or violating Scripture or conscience just to keep various factions happy.

A fear-dominated culture in any organization cannot and will not please the Lord. I believe the reason leaders and followers fall into the "pleasing man" rather than "pleasing God" mind-set is because there is a culture of fear in the group or organization rather than a culture of openness and candor. When not upsetting anyone (especially the big givers and the dominant leaders) is an unwritten law, a culture of walking gingerly and always looking over one's shoulder develops over time.

But a culture where the opinions, views, ideas, dreams, and convictions of leaders as well as the opinions of followers can be shared will do much to help us focus on living for an audience of one! We should all desire a culture where everyone is focused on a common purpose, direction, and vision, rather than focused on strong-willed personalities.

I like Eugene Peterson's paraphrase of Proverbs 29:25: "The fear of human opinion disables; trusting in God protects you from that" (MESSAGE). By God's grace we so need protection from the fear of human opinion. In the end we stand before the Lord and him alone. We are answerable to him and him alone, not to a parent, a spouse, a leader, a team, or a board.

> Jesus, I confess that I have been more concerned with what others think about me and my ministry than with what you think. I have been living in fear, and I have been a slave to other people's opinions. Help me by your grace to hear your voice above the din of so many other voices, and grant me the courage to obey you and the willingness to be unpopular if that's what is necessary.

FOOD FOR THOUGHT

1. List some of the people whose opinion you fear. Why is this so? Have you ever discussed this with them? If not, why not?
2. What is it in your own upbringing, background, or personality that keeps you so intent on pleasing everybody?
3. If you were guaranteed success and money were not an issue, what one thing would you attempt that you have been afraid to try because of your fear of human opinion?
4. Who on your team have personalities similar to Chris's? What can you do to pastor them so that fear of people's opinions doesn't damage their ministries?

5

ALLOWING BUSYNESS TO REPLACE VISIONING

Busyness is the new spirituality.—Fred Smith

As I look around me, it seems that most leaders are moving too fast and trying to do too much. There is precious little time set aside to think, pray, plan, and listen to the Lord. In the West we function with a "faster, better, bigger" mind-set in most Christian leadership settings. We equate busyness with spirituality. The tech toys we use create constant connectivity and compete with the serious praying, thinking, and planning times we so desperately need in order to lead well. Author Fred Smith says that busyness is the new spirituality!

THE STORY

Many women have leadership roles at CCC, but Suzie was the only woman on the leadership team. She was in her mid-fifties, married with teenage children, and responsible for both the children's ministry and women's ministry. Suzie had always been a doer, the Martha of team Mary and Martha. Because of her great people skills and ability to get things done, which always impressed Norm, she had quickly been given a major leadership role and joined the executive team. In hindsight this had not been a good decision. Good doers don't necessarily make good leaders.

Suzie has a heart of gold, wanted to be there for anyone who needed her, and tended to ignore the principle of Sabbath in order to get things done and love the people she felt responsible for. Her husband, Carl (an engineer), is a quiet sort of guy and loves Jesus, but is not the outgoing, energetic, be everywhere, do everything type of person that Suzie is.

They make a good team in one sense, as she is more outgoing and he is more introspective. He likes to think and plan and Suzie likes to do and go. But Suzie's ministry description clearly stated that she was to manage the day-to-day activities and programs of both the women's and children's ministry *as well as plan strategically with her team for the future.* Suzie was good at the day to day, but never got around to the thinking, planning, and future visioning. She was good with a microscope but not with the telescope.

Pastor Jim (to whom she reported) loved that Suzie was so good at taking care of the details for events that she had in front of her as well as shepherding her direct reports, but he noticed that she always seemed to be behind in thinking about what was next and creating a sense of vision. At heart she loved the nuts and bolts of ministry, but sitting down in front of her computer calendar and peering into the future left her cold—she actually despised it. The Martha inside of her rebelled, and she felt as if she were wasting her time.

She had the same problem on the home front. It was easy to do the thing in front of her while ignoring the future. This frustrated her husband and kids, but they just acclimated themselves to it. Carl was the planner at work and at home as well, to offset Suzie's penchant for the tyranny of the urgent and inattention to long-term, often more important things.

At church, Pastor Jim had tried a number of things to encourage Suzie to take time from the busy work of ministry to pray, think, and plan into the next year or two. She was given books and articles to read, and the church even sent her to conferences that focused on how to be a strategic leader. She would try for a while, but then slip back into her old habits. She honestly didn't see her own weaknesses, and felt she was doing just fine in her ministry assignments. Others didn't agree.

Suzie had a kind heart, was a hard worker, and deeply cared about those under her care, but the lack of personal discipline in taking time from her "busyness" to think and plan ahead was hurting her and others more than she realized. She didn't understand how her lack of planning and visioning hurt the morale of her children's and women's ministry teams. Her direct reports felt she didn't really care about their ministry because she made no effort to help them create vision for the future. She didn't encourage them to set goals, which could have created excitement and increased morale.

After one disastrous month during which just about all of her key people from both women and children's ministry came to Jim with complaints that Suzie perhaps was in the wrong role, things became more serious. Her people began to lose respect and trust in her leadership. Suzie was a good worker, but not a good leader. She could get things done, but she didn't know (or didn't want to know) how to get a vision from the Lord, cast that vision, communicate that vision regularly, and inspire her teams to move toward that shared vision.

The bottom line was that she was either not really a leader at all, but just a good worker, or that she didn't see the need to grow in becoming a strategic and visionary leader, which her role called for.

Suzie's lack of strategic planning and thinking had reached crisis mode!

It was Jim's responsibility to handle the issue of low morale among those in Suzie's ministry realm, before they started to check out and leave. He had already done all he knew how to do in expressing how important it was for Suzie to give adequate time to planning and visioning about the future. The book assignments, articles, and conferences didn't seem to make a bit of difference. In retrospect, Jim realized that Suzie was not a good fit for her visioning responsibilities, and she should not have been hired for that role.

It was time for the "come to Jesus" talk. It would not be easy for Jim, because everyone knew and loved Suzie as a person and as a CCC member. Talking to Suzie about the state of her ministry was one of the toughest assignments that Jim had ever had in his role as executive pastor. Suzie and her family were a fixture at CCC, and letting her go could potentially have negative consequences for those close to her family. Her family had been part of the church since it had been founded.

Jim had multiple conversations with Suzie over the course of a few months. In their last conversation he kindly but frankly told her that her job was in jeopardy if he and Norm didn't see some major progress in her ability to plan and think toward the future. In one sense Suzie wasn't completely surprised, but she didn't really believe that they would actually let her go, because of her family's long history with the church, their strong financial support of CCC, and that they were deeply loved by so many.

After Suzie continued to show an unwillingness to change, Jim met with her one more time. He stated the facts carefully and firmly. He had spent much time in prayer. He did not want to be cruel or insensitive in the way he handled the situation. But it was time for Suzie to go. He again told her how much the church valued her contributions over the years both as a worker in the children's ministry and as a vital part of the women's ministry, but that her lack of creating vision and direction for both of her teams was not acceptable in her current assignment.

Jim expressed his sadness, but was firm that she needed to step down within thirty days, and they would be looking for her replacement. This stunned Suzie, but not Carl. He reasoned to himself that a person at his engineering firm who had functioned like Suzie would have been let go much sooner.

There were tears at home that evening, but Suzie also felt some relief. She was more than welcomed, and needed, as a worker and servant in ministry, but not as a leader.

PRINCIPLE AND PRACTICE

There is a world of difference between management and biblical leadership. Management is caring for the here and now, whereas biblical leadership is concerned with the there and coming. Management deals with what is, and biblical leadership deals with what could be. Many ministries are overmanaged and underled. Vision inspires and motivates people to accomplish what pleases the Lord. Without seeing the bigger picture of the future, people tend to lose sight and lose heart. In hindsight, Suzie should have never been given the role she had without demonstrating that she was willing, and able, to learn how to be a visionary leader for children's and women's ministries. This was clearly a leadership oversight.

She made the tragic mistake of replacing future visioning with busyness, and she paid the price in the loss of her job. Norm and Jim had a tough decision to make. Fortunately their heads went before their hearts, but not without heart. Suzie either had to go, or her team members would begin leaving.

Every true leader needs to operate with the microscope of things up close and the telescope of things far off. I have known countless young visionary leaders on church staffs that are led by pastors who are good teachers, administrators, and counselors, but who do not have a visionary bone in their bodies. Leaders of ministries need to be visionaries, or they should let somebody else lead. They need to always be thinking about the future.

I love what Marcus Buckingham says about this:

> What defines a leader is his preoccupation with the future. He is a leader if, and only if, he is able to rally others to the better future he sees . . . my point is simply that leaders are fascinated by the future. You are a leader if, and only if, you are restless for change, impatient for progress and deeply dissatisfied with the status quo. I am not satisfied, this is the mantra of the leader. As a leader you are never satisfied with the present, because in your head you can see a better future. Whenever a person strives to make other see a better future, there is leadership . . . you do it because you can't help it. You do it because you see the future so vividly, so distinctly that you can't get it out of your head.[1]

I say it again: biblical leadership is concerned with the future, while management is concerned with the present. Our God is a God of the future. He is leading his people and his leaders to a desired destination he has for all of us, individually and corporately.

Visionary leadership is all about impacting our communities and the world with the gospel of the good news about Jesus and helping Christians become fully devoted disciples of Jesus. True leadership is always forward thinking and forward moving. Leadership is all about taking people from where they are to where they could be, following a desirable God-given vision for the future.

I spend a lot of time coaching leaders around the country. The biggest concern I hear from those on a pastoral team who are not the lead pastor is that their church has no vision for the future, and people are drifting away and loosing heart and motivation. It is not enough for leaders to focus only on the present, as Suzie did. They must also plan, think, and dream about what is not yet at hand but what could be—with the grace of God! Biblical leadership requires taking time to be in God's presence often enough to hear from him what he wants to do in the future in your church, ministry, or group.

I am a doer by nature. I can fully identify with Suzie. I love to be active, accomplish things, and check things off on my to-do list. I am much like Martha, and have to trust the Lord to develop Mary in my soul. If I don't set aside time for retreating to dream, think, plan, and pray, those things just don't happen. I am active, restless, and want to keep busy, but my active mind and spirit can be my worst enemies.

I believe that a leader's primary responsibility is to hear from God. Leaders are to listen to what God wants to accomplish through them in the future. Am I to build something like Noah or Nehemiah? Am I to lead people from point A to point B like Moses and Joshua? Am I to plant new ministries like Paul? Am I to step out in faith with deep conviction like Esther?

A leader will make time for what is immediately at hand, but not to the detriment of peering into the future and painting a picture for followers of what could be. I spent eight years as a missionary in Sweden. Sweden, as well as much of the rest of Europe, is covered with museums that were once vibrant churches. When a ministry or church has no visionary leaders and when leaders are content with only managing and improving what is already happening, the ministry likely will not last.

There were once two seriously ill men who shared a small room in a large hospital. This small room had one window looking out on the world. One of the men, as part of his treatment, was allowed to sit up in his bed for an hour every afternoon. His bed was next to the window. But the other man had to spend all his time flat on his back.

Every afternoon when the man next to the window was propped up, he would pass the time by describing to his roommate what he could see outside. The window overlooked a park with a lake. Ducks and swans swam in the lake, and children came to throw them bread and sail model boats. Young lovers walked hand in hand beneath the trees. Behind the fringe of trees was a fine view of the city skyline.

The man on his back would listen to the other man describe all of this, enjoying every minute. He heard how a child nearly fell into the lake, and how beautiful the girls were in their summer dresses. His friend's descriptions almost made him feel as if he were the one looking out the window. Then one fine afternoon, the thought struck him: Why should the man next to the window have all the pleasure of seeing what was going on? Why shouldn't he get the chance? He felt ashamed, but the more he tried not to think like that, the worse he wanted a change. He'd do anything!

One night as he stared at the ceiling, the other man suddenly woke up, coughing and choking, his hands groping for the button that would bring the nurse running. But the man who was flat on his back did nothing—even when the sound of his roommate's breathing stopped. In the morning, the nurse found the other man dead, and she quietly took his body away. As soon as it seemed decent, the man asked if he could be switched to the bed next to the window. So the nurses moved him, tucked him in, and made him quite comfortable. The minute they left, he propped himself up on one elbow, painfully and laboriously, and looked out the window.

It faced a blank wall!

What do you see as you gaze out the window of your imagination? Have you lost your ability to dream and imagine for the glory of God? Are you so involved with present activities that you see no future possibilities? As a leader you can't afford to be so engrossed with the present that you have no time for the future.

> Jesus, I confess my sin of busyness and of equating it with spirituality. Forgive me for being so active that I am not getting a fresh word from you. Show me what you want to accomplish in the future with my life and the lives of those I am privileged to lead. Help me to slow down and listen to your still, small voice.

FOOD FOR THOUGHT

1. Are you more of a doer or more of a visionary?
2. Look at your calendar. Do you have specific time set aside to get away to hear from God? What has he been telling you or showing you?
3. Can you articulate for the people you lead what you are hearing from the Lord regarding the future?
4. What can you do to be less like Martha and more like Mary?
5. If you spot Suzie-like traits in a person on your team, how can you effectively lead this person toward change?

6

ALLOWING FINANCIAL FRUGALITY TO REPLACE FEARLESS FAITH

Ships are safe in the harbor,
but that's not why ships are built.

When financial decisions are made, what one person views as faith, by taking somewhat of a risk, someone else views as an act of stupidity or carelessness. On staff teams, people who want to make healthy financial-risk decisions are often in tension with those who see the same decision as foolish and unwarranted. Some churches are on good financial footing, but are not growing and reaching out with fresh vision and exciting dreams. They are safe in the harbor. Others are taking some reasonable financial risks and seeing God do some amazing things. We need to be willing to take healthy risks, but it's not always easy to tell the difference between good risks and potentially bad risks. When life is over, for leaders and their churches, we will probably have more regrets over what we did not do than what we did do. We will be mostly guilty of sins of omission, not sins of commission. Fear of failure might win over steps of faith! One of the reasons many churches stay small is that they are afraid to take faith risks and trust the One who can do the impossible.

THE STORY

Bob came to CCC after thirty years as an officer in the Marines. His entire military career was spent in the financial arena. After retirement, he and his wife, Shirley, decided to move back to Northern California, where they had both originally come from. Bob had plenty of time on his hands, and with his extensive background in finances, he soon landed a job as the church's director of finance. After a year or two in this role, Bob also became one of the elders. He did an excellent job of putting together the budget each year and making sure expenses stayed on track, as well as cutting back when offerings didn't meet expectations. He was, however, a bit too conservative for CCC, and he became even more so as time progressed.

As a retired Marine, Bob could be a little too authoritative and brusque at times, but for the most part people in general and the staff in particular got along with him . . . at least in the beginning. Bob was interesting in a number of ways. He was the oldest member of the leadership team. He was the only ex-military member (but a Marine will bristle when called an ex-Marine). He had the most experience and expertise in financial matters, and he was definitely someone who got things done. Perhaps he was not as gracious and sensitive as he could have been, but Norm in particular was glad to have him around because he took a liking to staff members who "got 'er done."

A few years into his eldership and staff position as director of finance (with no salary due to a nice retirement from the military), a shift began to take place. Many on the team thought that Bob was becoming a little more gruff and that he seemed to focus on the bottom line more than the people CCC was trying to reach and disciple. Over time, Bob came to believe that his primary role was to curb new ideas and protect the finances rather than be a "can-do player" that could figure out ways to make new ideas happen.

The pocketbook was taking precedence over the people. More and more staff people were hitting a wall with Bob when it came to funding new initiatives, even though the money was there to spend. Bob wanted to create increasingly safe margins (i.e., a fat savings account). He saw himself as responsible for deciding what got spent and what didn't, a role he was never actually assigned. Because of his authoritative demeanor, it was not easy to have reasonable discussions with him. Bob usually won any arguments about finances at CCC. Helping CCC be financially secure had taken over in Bob's decision-making values. People were no longer a high priority for him.

When the pastoral staff met without Bob present, it was clear the problem with Bob was getting worse, but what should they do? Most of his fellow elders had no idea he was at odds with the rest of the staff and pastors and actually appreciated what Bob took responsibility for (particularly since the church was saving thousands of dollars a year by not needing to hire an accountant). Bob didn't need the money that a salary would give him, but he definitely liked the position and authority he assumed he had.

He and Pastor Norm did have one thing in common, though: keeping an eye on the bottom line. Norm's bottom line was the number of people involved at CCC; Bob's bottom line was dollars. Eventually, the number of dollars became at odds with the number of people. Norm wanted to spend money on things that would bring more people in; Bob wanted to hang on to as much money as possible, regardless of ministry needs. A war was on, and it had outcomes that few could have predicted.

Norm and his pastoral team (Jim, Jason, and Brent) were increasingly frustrated with Bob's attitude and argumentative nature whenever the subject of finances came up. They all agreed that too much was in savings and not enough was being invested in new initiatives. They agreed that a certain amount should be saved on a regular basis, but it seemed to them that Bob's mind-set had gone from savings to hording. The team believed that this was a clear violation of numerous passages in the book of Proverbs, as well as Jesus's clear teaching in Matthew 6 and Paul's words on finances in 1 Timothy 6.

To make some changes, the pastoral team would have to involve the rest of the elders. The right thing to do would be to let Bob go, but the financially prudent thing to do would be to work around him rather than replace him. This discussion (held mainly between Norm and Jim) went on for many weeks. Letting Bob go would be expensive and could cause some issues with the other elders. Keeping him would mean continuing in the constant battles between him and the staff.

Before a decision could be made, the most amazing thing happened.

On his own initiative, Bob came to Norm and said he was leaving his position as finance director, his eldership, and the church. Norm's jaw dropped in obvious outward disbelief, but also inward joy! As Norm and Bob sat in Norm's office, he couldn't believe what he was hearing. He had to restrain himself from jumping up and singing the "Hallelujah" chorus. Norm listened with no expression, but inside he was beside himself with joy. The fears of having to talk with Bob and possibly remove him had added years to Norm's life and not a few gray hairs. A memo quickly went out to the staff, and within a week word was on the website and in the Sunday announcements, and the hunt was on for a replacement. Fortunately, there were no issues with CCC for Bob and Shirley. They had simply decided they needed to move to be closer to their kids and grandkids who lived in Arizona. And just like that they were gone, accompanied by a corporate sigh of relief from the staff.

PRINCIPLE AND PRACTICE

Norm and the staff at CCC learned a great deal from their experience with Bob, and they did a much better job on interviews in the future. The decision before them (had Bob not decided to move on) had been a tough one. Having value alignment among the staff took on a whole new meaning for CCC. Bob would certainly not be the only person in ministry whose financial frugality did more harm than help for the kingdom. The war between these two competing values is akin to the worship wars that in many quarters are still being fought.

I believe it was Peter Drucker who said that efficiency is doing things right, but being effective is doing the right things.

Identifying the right thing to do in a situation such as this is not always simple. And once you have identified the best thing to do, it can be difficult to implement when you are trying to take healthy and appropriate faith risks while at the same time striving to be financially prudent and wise. Every church I have ever been a part of has struggled with this balance.

In Bob's case, CCC's first mistake was hiring him without having asked enough questions to see if his financial values aligned with the financial values of CCC. Bob valued financial security over reaching people for Jesus—so much so that he was willing to hinder the church from doing things to reach and disciple people.

I have been in churches and coached people in other churches where an elder or two were trying to protect the church from the staff. This is never a good situation. When you lose trust in your leaders, everything is downhill from there. In far too many cases just a few people hold the pastoral team hostage when it comes to taking appropriate steps of faith to advance the kingdom and the gospel. I have also seen foolish and presumptive steps of so-called faith-taking that have caused churches to come to a standstill, resulting in budget cuts and staff layoffs.

A few years ago, when you drove up the middle of California, you could see the shell of a church building that never got finished. I asked somebody who lived in the area what had happened. This particular church had borrowed lots of money to erect a new facility and didn't have the money to pay back the loan, so construction had stopped. There sat this partly finished worship facility as a reminder to all who drove by of the story Jesus told about people who didn't count the cost before beginning to build, and were not able to finish what they started.

I believe it is the role of the top leadership in a church or organization to cast vision in such a way that the people are excited to step in and step up financially to make it happen. I have come to believe that people give to vision more than to programs or buildings. Where there is visionary leadership there also needs to be good vision casting and fundraising. When things get tight, you can either cut back or raise more funds. In my opinion it is always better to raise money than to cut back.

Churches in particular would be wise to have good processes in place and to think through how they will fund their vision over the long term. We must avoid operating in crisis mode (which happens when we spend beyond our means), which often results in drastically cutting back and laying off when funds are not forthcoming.

For several years I was part of a church staff that really figured this out. The income was seasonal, so we built the budget accordingly and saved for the lean months during the fat months (like the fat cows/skinny cows that we find in Exodus during Joseph's leadership). All leadership teams need members who are both faith-filled and financially wise, not one or the other.

I personally don't think Scripture precludes a church from borrowing money, as long as it can afford to repay the loan without scuttling its faith initiatives in advancing the gospel and discipling their own. Some churches refuse to borrow and are consequently never able to take any faith steps. Borrowing is not the problem, but borrowing more than you can pay back is.

Before my experience in the fat-cow/skinny-cow church, I was part of a fairly large church that had no budget at all and no idea of how much money was coming in or going out. The lead pastor had no systems in place for much of anything, and the church got into big financial trouble. The pastor, his brother, and his sister ran the finances, and nobody (including the three of them) had a clue what was going on.

So we have some churches that have lots of money in the bank and are financially secure, but are unwilling to spend money to reach lost people and see them mature in their faith. On the other hand we have churches that have borrowed too much and are living extravagantly, until they run into trouble with banks and church members who had no idea things were so bad. I love the wisdom of Ecclesiastes 7:18: "It is good to grasp the one and not let go of the other. The man who fears God will avoid all extremes" (NIV). We want to avoid the extremes of faithless frugality and presumptuous faith.

Various experts on financial issues host seminars all over the country that are helpful for both individuals and families. I don't know of a lot of such seminars that are for churches. What churches generally do when they are in financial trouble or want to do something on a large scale is to hire an organization to work with them over several months on how to raise capital funds. If churches and Christian organizations would adhere to a few simple principles, perhaps they wouldn't get themselves in dire straits that mandate paying thousands of dollars to hire an outside consultant.

Here are a few basic principles that can help churches avoid unhealthy financial frugality and be in a position to act on biblically based, fearless faith.

1. *Understand that the Lord himself is our resource.* We belong to God and are not our own, nor are we the owners of the resources we have, but stewards of what he owns. We manage—we don't own—and we will give an account to the Owner some day.

2. *Develop a philosophy of our standard of living (spending).* Many groups and churches have no written and agreed-upon documents that spell out what they believe about allocating the resources God provides. Organizations seldom have written and agreed-upon val-

ues and procedures, but they often have many arguments and turf wars over who gets how much and for what reason.

3. *Balance income, saving, giving, and spending.* Just like a person or a family would divide the dispensing of funds into the three categories of giving, saving, and spending, I suggest that churches do likewise. Perhaps churches should apply the 80/10/10 principle of spending 80 percent, giving 10 percent, and saving 10 percent.

Many churches that are in trouble spend 110 percent of their income and do so via credit cards and lines of credit. They are always anticipating that the next Sunday (or a few Sundays from now), some big gifts will come in that will enable them to catch up. Some churches put too much stock in year-end giving in December to help them get back into the black; some even preach and pound people to give toward the end of the year. Then when that doesn't happen, the church must start a new year off with cutbacks and layoffs—not a good way to keep morale and vision up for a brand new year.

Most churches don't save much or give much either. The bottom line is that a lot of churches are materialistic and spend entirely too much money on the wrong things that hinder them from their true calling to evangelize and disciple. Hebrews 13:5 is a good reminder: "Keep your life free from love of money, and be content with what you have, for he has said, 'I will never leave you nor forsake you.'"

4. *Make financial decisions a team effort.* Don't let big outlays of money be the decision of One powerful personality. Whether he be frugal or faith-filled, he should never make big financial decisions on his own. Have a team of people who see things from different points of view so healthy decisions are made.

> Jesus, help us to have faith to step out and believe that your work done in your way will not lack your provision. Keep us from being either safe in the harbor or shipwrecked at sea because we have not trusted you and handled the finances in a way that honors you. Thank you for your promise to supply our needs as we seek to know you and make you known to a needy world all around us.

FOOD FOR THOUGHT

1. Is your church (or organization) fear-filled or a faith-filled when it comes to finances?
2. Do you need to spend more or save more?
3. Do you have a wise person (or team) overseeing your finances or is your budget out of control?
4. How much of your income do you give to advance the gospel in other locales?
5. Is there a Bob in your midst? How does Jesus want you to help him?

7

ALLOWING ARTIFICIAL HARMONY TO REPLACE DIFFICULT CONFLICT

Constructive conflict is difficult but
essential for healthy teams and organizations.

Harry Truman said, "If you can't stand the heat, get out of the kitchen." Leadership is first and foremost about tackling tough issues and making hard decisions. I have seen pastors leave churches rather than deal with difficult people or difficult issues. But Ephesians 4:15 admonishes us to speak the truth in love. We are not to be so loving that we don't speak the truth, or so truthful that we don't speak with love; there is a fine balance between the two that is essential to all human relationships, especially among church staff and in a leadership role.

THE STORY
Bryan had been involved in music as far back as his family could remember. He took a liking to both the piano and guitar at a young

age, played in the high school band, and even had his own little group that did gigs around town when he was in high school. His family had attended CCC from the start, and Bryan grew up in the church and became a Christian at a junior high summer camp.

He was a quiet young man, but he was a faithful and steady plodder in whatever he undertook, and he had a heart of gold, which opened many doors of opportunity for him. Bryan was not a serious student, so rather than going to college, he choose to work in a local music store and give guitar lessons on the side to pay for his part of the cost for the small house he shared with two other guys from CCC. Bryan didn't have what anyone would call strong leadership gifts, but he had matured into a solid worship leader, and some people thought he might eventually become the worship pastor. CCC gave him a small monthly stipend for his part-time work with music at the church.

Bryan was able to spot good talent and he was organized enough to keep things on track from week to week. At age twenty-four, he was doing pretty well. He was still single, but he was definitely interested in getting married some day (he was not pursuing anyone, although several young ladies in the church were hoping he would pursue them). Bryan's time was taken up with music. He continued to do gigs, and this along with his job at the music store and his responsibilities for leading worship at CCC took most of his time. His folks had friends in the church who tried to play matchmaker, but Bryan was not quite ready yet.

If Bryan had one downside, it was that he didn't like conflict and wanted everybody to get along and be a big happy family. Since some (but not all) musicians are prone to being independent and having out-of-the box ideas, Bryan was challenged regularly in dealing with conflicts originating from his own team, as well as from members of the congregation who had their own ideas on worship.

Other than letting Bryan know what the sermon topic would be each week, Pastor Norm pretty much left the oversight of Bryan to

Pastor Jim. But Jim had his hands full with Jason, Chris, and Brent (whom we'll meet in the next chapter), as well as finding a replacement for both Suzie and Bob. Jim well understood the importance of the Sunday worship experience at CCC and how highly attenders valued it, next to the sermon. Jim saw in Bryan great musical talent, a love for people, an outstanding walk with Jesus, and a solid understanding of the gospel that shone through all he did on Sundays with his team.

But in the back of Jim's mind, he was concerned about whether Bryan had the moxie to strongly lead the team well and get tough when toughness was called for. Jim had been around long enough to know that a person who was good at performing well at individual tasks was not necessarily able to lead others in a team context. Could Bryan really (in a few years) step into the role of full-time worship pastor? Bryan was younger than some of those on his team, and he was not a strong personality type, which made it easy for strong ones to challenge him and potentially create conflict. And Bryan definitely did not like conflict.

Jim spent a lot of time with Bryan to help him grow into his role. They talked about convictions, spiritual authority, and what it meant to hear from Jesus and cast vision for Bryan's team. In some of their times together, Jim had the two of them do some role playing to learn how to deal with overly opinioned congregants and team members. They studied some material on teams, with an emphasis on dealing with conflict. Jim had faced similar challenges with Chris, whom we met in chapter 4, and the Holy Spirit did a great work of grace in Chris's heart and leadership. Jim was trusting that he would see similar spiritual growth in Bryan.

Bryan and Chris were actually good friends and connected outside of work. Neither Chris nor Bryan were high-powered, dynamic leader types, but both loved the gospel and walked solidly with Jesus. They at times discussed being tougher as leaders when necessary—not mean or disrespectful to people, just tougher.

Jim began to wonder whether conflict resolution was a skill people could learn, or if there were certain personality types that were just not capable of dealing with conflict well. It appeared that highly relational types had a much more difficult time with it (both Chris and Bryan fell into this category), whereas Norm and Jason almost enjoyed conflict. Jim increasingly understood that if Bryan couldn't change his leadership skills in the area of conflict resolution, he would probably not be able to grow into more significant responsibility. He would be able to lead worship from time to time and play at special events, but a top leadership role would not be in his future.

Certain members of Bryan's worship team (there were several different groupings of musicians) challenged him regularly on his preferences, choices, and style. Bryan knew he needed to hold his ground, but it was so hard, and the confrontations tied his stomach in knots. He felt increasing pressure (real or imagined) to do things differently, until he finally got to where he no longer enjoyed the role as worship director. Finally he and Jim decided it would be best if Bryan were relieved of his leadership responsibilities and instead be content with being a part of one of the worship bands. It was agreed that a search would begin for someone a little older and more experienced that could step into the role of worship pastor.

Jim was both frustrated and disappointed that things didn't work out with Bryan. Jim was convinced that Bryan could have become a true leader, but that he simply was not willing to do what was so difficult for him. Jim still thinks about how easy it is to create a superficial harmony that belies conflicts, and that either intentionally buries problems or overlooks them because someone just doesn't want to deal with uncomfortable situations. Jim still does not know if the root cause of such problems is sin, particular personalities, fear of some sort, gifting, or something he has not yet identified. Whatever it is, it kept Bryan from reaching his full potential as a leader.

Jim had been glad to see Bob step aside, but he felt differently about Bryan. Fortunately Bryan had a good attitude about the whole thing, remained at CCC, eventually found that gal, and continued teaching guitar lessons and working at the music store. But Jim never fully recovered from the sense of what might have been. There was so much he liked about Bryan, compared with so much he had disliked about Jason.

PRINCIPLE AND PRACTICE

A pastor once explained to me that he was under a lot of stress, as were the other pastors of this multistaffed church. "If you were here," he told me, "we would have let him [a staffer who wasn't working out] go a long time ago, but it seems that nobody has the courage to deal with it." Another close friend was in conflict with a person at work. He told me that when things are going smoothly with people, he gets along famously, but when he collides or is in ongoing conflict with somebody, he doesn't know what to do. He asked if I could give him some advice. I could see the stress, frustration, and pain he was experiencing.

A few years ago, I got a phone call from a good friend who had applied for a new assignment within the large organization for which he worked. He told me that the regional manager decided to change the role (and the rules) to make this job a rotating position rather than a permanent assignment. My friend would have the job for six months and then go back to his present assignment. Somebody else would rotate in for six months and then back to his previous slot. I told him it was my understanding that he had applied for this job as a new full-time position.

He had, but the boss had decided not to offer it as such because a certain individual in the organization with seniority would apply, and they didn't want that person to have the job. The boss in question had worked with this person before and didn't want to do it again, so he changed the rules and the assignment to keep him from applying. The boss was confident that the person wouldn't apply for the job because of the six-month rotation requirement. My friend told me that the "difficult person" in question was somewhat lazy, didn't have a good work ethic, and was generally difficult to work with. I asked the obvious question: Hadn't anybody ever dealt with this person by confronting his behavior and work ethic? Nobody had had the courage to do that—not the present boss or anybody else during this person's tenure with the company.

As I sat in amazement after the phone call, I thought of the many times I had seen this in my years of leadership. I have come to the conclusion that many leaders would rather leave their organization, change rules (as in the case described above), lie, or do almost anything rather than confront people or issues that need to be dealt with.

I was on a team years ago where the leader was totally incompetent and everybody knew it, including the leader himself and our regional leader. It was well within the authority of the regional leader to dismiss or at least confront this person and suggest alternative jobs, but instead he created a team to compensate for the person's inabilities, and kept him around. After a year or so he was finally let go, but it should have happened much earlier. It would have been the best for all concerned. But the courage was not there.

What is lacking in the above situations, and numerous others I have experienced and read about, is courageous leadership—the willingness to make the tough decisions; the courage to do the right thing, which may not always be the popular thing; and the courage not to plan around the person or the issue. I have seen this tendency toward avoidance in churches, in Christian organizations, in politics, in the military, and in many business settings. People fear litigation or recrimination, making an unpopular decision, or being disliked by peers. People also fear losing money, position, or power.

Not knowing how and/or being unwilling to deal with conflict is a major issue that is undermining organizations today. I run into this problem everywhere I go; the examples above could be multiplied many times over. I cannot imagine anything more devastating to effective leadership than the refusal or inability to resolve conflict. To be frank, I meet very few leaders who honestly, gracefully, and promptly deal with conflict. I don't mean this to be unkind, but many leaders are "relational cowards."

Sometimes the reason people give for not dealing with conflict is, "I don't want to be unloving." What? Not dealing with conflict is the unloving thing to do. Away with the mistaken idea that love is never conflicting with a person or never resolving conflicts. As Bill Hybels says:

> Truth telling is more important than peacekeeping . . . the well-being of the other person is more important than the current comfort level in the relationship . . . peace at any price is a form of deception from the pit of hell. A relationship built on peacekeeping won't last. Tough love chooses truth telling over peace keeping and trusts God for the results.[1]

Let me set the record straight before I go on. I am not an expert on this subject. I have had my share of cowardly moments for which I have paid dearly. I will more than likely have a few more before Jesus calls me home. I strongly desire to and will (with dependence on God's grace) no longer sweep conflict under the carpet or look the other way. Ignoring conflict is unbiblical and shows lack of spiritual leadership and integrity. Having said that, allow me to share some things that help me cope with conflict.

1. *Make a commitment before the Lord to face and deal honestly, lovingly, sensitively, and decisively* with conflict. For years I carried a card with me that said, "Courage and conviction to collide and confront." It was a reminder to me to be courageous and not back down too fast when I collided with people on issues, or when (after prayer, thought, and counsel) I decided I needed to take the initiative and confront someone.

2. *Be prepared to confess and ask for forgiveness for your part* in

causing the conflict. I want to begin by acknowledging my part in causing the seeming impasse in the relationship. I don't do this so that the other party will confess his part, but because I, usually without realizing it, have probably contributed to the conflict

3. *Get all the facts.* When I am handling conflict correctly, I ask lots of questions, without accusing or placing blame. Demonstrate a sincere desire to get to the bottom of the conflict by listening and trying to understand.

4. *Do it privately.* The rule of thumb is, confront privately, praise publicly. Never confront or air a conflict (for the first time) in public. Matthew 18 gives us the process to follow. I have actually seen a brother or sister be confronted in a church service or a staff meeting.

I am honestly not sure if replacing difficult conflict with superficial harmony is a sin or a serious mistake, but both my personal experience and the experience I have had in working with churches and in coaching leaders around the country makes it clear that it is definitely a leadership problem that, if not faced, has serious consequences for individual leaders as well as the churches, groups, or organizations they have been tasked to lead. Recall Luke 6:26: "Woe to you, when all people speak well of you, for so their fathers did to the false prophets."

A number of years ago I consulted with a church and worked with its wonderfully gifted pastor, who was an excellent communicator, a good team builder, and a Jesus-loving, gospel-centered leader. He had one man on his elder board that had it in for him (this was in a church that has close to a thousand people worshiping on Sundays). I asked the pastor what he was going to do about this. To my shock he said he was seriously considering leaving the church. "You can't be serious?" I asked him. But he was very serious.

Ready to leave a church over a conflict with a single individual? I asked if he had tried to sit down and talk with this gentleman. He had not and he had no intention of doing so. This elder was the white elephant in the room of many staff meetings. I would love to say this was the first, last, and only time I have seen this kind of situation—unfortunately it is not.

We must be aware that replacing difficult conflict with artificial harmony is a serious sin/mistake that can cause real problems within our organizations.

> Jesus, I confess that many times I am a coward when it comes to dealing biblically with conflict. I admit it is difficult to trust you with the outcomes of speaking the truth in love. Please help me, by your Spirit, to be more interested in what you think than about what others may think if I choose to engage in necessary confrontations. Give me Holy Spirit boldness to speak out.

FOOD FOR THOUGHT

1. Can you identify a person you have avoided because you have refused to talk honestly with him or her about issues?
2. When will you have that talk?
3. Do you have a volunteer or staff person who has been causing problems for years, but whom no one is willing to confront?
4. What issue or problem in your group or church needs to be faced head-on and dealt with for the sake of the gospel?
5. What can you do, with God's help, to come alongside of the Bryans and help them grow in being courageous?

8

ALLOWING PERENNIALLY HURTING PEOPLE TO REPLACE POTENTIAL HUNGRY LEADERS

The primary role of a leader is to develop leaders.

Without a doubt this chapter will be the most controversial and receive the most push back. For any ministry to grow and be healthy, it is paramount that the leader balance his time between different kinds of people. The primary responsibility of a leader is to develop additional leaders so as not to be continually over-whelmed as the ministry grows. If all the leader's time is devoted to shepherding and counseling hurting people to the exclusion of nurturing hungry future leaders, the ministry cannot continue to grow as God would desire. And there is a good chance the leaders will eventually burn themselves out.

THE STORY

Brent is clearly the priest on the team. His heart has always gone out to the hurting, those with really harmful backgrounds, traumatic experiences, and dysfunctional families. Long before he stepped into the role of pastor of counseling and support groups, most of his time went to hurting people. His wife, Patty, was gifted and passionate in the very much the same ways.

Their time and their home were largely filled with those who needed a lot of love and encouragement, accompanied by listening ears and a tender heart. They loved people and doing whatever they could for them, particularly helping them discover their identity in Christ and encouraging them to stay centered on him, not the hurt and harm from the past. It takes time to help people see that their past pain doesn't need to define them, but that their identity in Jesus (what he did for them on the cross and through his resurrection) is what defines them.

As Norm and Jim, along with other staff people, observed Brent and Patty in action, it seemed clear to them that Brent would be ideal for overseeing the support group and counseling ministries. They were semiretired, empty nesters with both time and heart for such a role.

This is a common leadership error I have mentioned elsewhere in this book—promoting someone who is good at doing something and assuming that they will also be good at overseeing others doing what they are good at, without requiring some additional training and experience. Brent had no experience overseeing and leading anything. He had been a high school counselor for most of his career, but never served in a leadership or management role.

Additionally, due to his deep care and concern for others, it was easy for him to neglect creating a team to share in those ministries. He naturally tended toward doing all of the counseling himself, with Patty pitching in with the women. His lack of experience coupled with other demands on his time made it likely that Brent would not last long in his new role.

Let me clarify that Brent did possess leadership abilities; they just had never been developed. It was his lack of experience and need of ministry development that kept him from rising to his true potential as a leader. It wasn't that Brent and Patty didn't see the need to invest in others on their team and help them assume leadership roles. It was more that the needs of the hurting were so great and demanding that they never got around to investing in those with obvious leadership ability.

Much of the time, Brent and Patty were "leading on empty" and often fell into bed at midnight or later exhausted after giving out so much to so many day after day. As they were falling asleep, they would regularly have the conversation about needing to find and train others to help, but never seemed to get around to it or make it a priority due to so many other demands from the "hurting."

As with other staff, it fell to Executive Pastor Jim to deal with Brent and Patty's potential burn and the absence of new leaders being raised up in the counseling and support group ministries. He had discussed this with Brent several times in the past and even put a note about the problem in his file. He had received heartfelt promises from Brent, but not much more. He hated the thought of yet another leader at CCC coming short of his true potential and the advancement of the gospel being truncated. He had prayed fervently about Brent and Patty's situation.

As he was preparing for one of his biweekly one-on-ones with Brent, Jim had an idea. As it turned out, it was not just a good idea, but a God idea. Jim decided to walk through the account of Moses and his father-in-law, Jethro, in Exodus 18. Sitting in Jim's office on a relatively slow Thursday, Jim and Brent opened their Bibles and began reading and discussing the visit Jethro paid to Moses (vv. 13–27). Jim reminded Brent that he and Moses shared something in common. Both saw themselves as the chief shepherd responsible for being available and meeting the needs of many people. Jim made a point of calling Brent's attention to the word "alone" in verses 14 and 18: "Why do you sit *alone*" and, "The thing is too heavy for you. You are not able to do it *alone*." They worked their way through the section, noting Jethro's emphasis on selecting others (v. 21), with Jethro describing these "others" whom Moses was to choose to help him carry the burden of the people. Moses was to select men who

- were able (competence);
- feared God (relationship with God);
- were trustworthy (character/relationships);
- hated a bribe (character/relationships); and
- were rulers of thousands, hundreds, fifties, and tens (capacity: gifting).

This was Brent's *aha!* moment. This is when his resolve and motivation kicked in!

Brent was empowered to connect the dots in his head and heart. He saw that giving so much time to the hurting while leaving no time for the hungry was sapping him and Patty of physical, spiritual, and emotional energy and health.

At that particular time, Brent happened to be reading *Leaders Who Last*. He saw similar admonitions in the chapters "The Leader's Pacing" and "The Leader's Influence." He happened to have his copy with him and turned to the pages where this issue is addressed. His eyes fell on Gordon McDonald's experience:

> I was making a serious mistake. Because the nice people were so pleasant to be with, and because the draining people requested so much time, I had little prime time left for the resourceful and the trainable people. None of the latter two made the demands upon me that the first two did. And I, because they made so few protests, left them alone as a rule because I thought I was where I was needed; an error of great magnitude.[1]

Tears began to fill Brent's eyes as it became clear how his actions were affecting Patty, those they were trying to help, and the potential leaders right under their noses whom they were ignoring and not investing in. Jim sat quietly praying with his arm resting gently on Brent's shoulder. Then he and Brent prayed together as Brent repented and confessed and with fresh resolve and dependency on the Holy Spirit headed home to talk with Patty about getting away for a day or two to rethink and reconfigure their ministry so that greater emphasis was on giving attention to the hungry potential leaders. By no means were they going to neglect the hurting, but they would need to do things differently to allow time for both the hurting and the hungry. This change would take a lot of time, along with personal discipline and intentionality, but Brent was ready to take on the challenge because so much was at stake.

Why hadn't he seen this more clearly before? He didn't really know. It was God's timing for him and his ministry. Jim breathed a sigh of relief that he didn't have another Suzie or Bryan on his hands, someone who wouldn't be able to see what needed to happen and do it. Jim even went so far as to promise Brent that he and Norm would do some thinking to see if they could find some people with strong mercy and shepherding gifts who were leader types and send them his way.

As Jim was driving home, he afresh understood and was grateful for the power of the Word of God in giving fuel to the Holy Spirit to use in having his way with his children. He vowed to use Scripture more in his ministry, being reminded of the promise in Hebrews 4:12: "For the word of God is living and active, sharper than any two-edged sword, piercing to the division of soul and of spirit, of joints and of marrow, and discerning the thoughts and intents of the heart." He also remembered Isaiah 55:11: "So shall my word be that goes out from my mouth; it shall not return to me empty, but it shall accomplish that which I purpose, and shall succeed in the thing for which I sent it."

PRINCIPLE AND PRACTICE

John Maxwell makes the observation that people with very strong mercy gifts don't function well in visionary leadership. They don't want to hurt anybody or make decisions that offend or cause conflict. My experience verifies that. Leaders who know they have a strong mercy side must be very careful about who they spend time with. All their available time and energy tends to go to the hurting and the discouraged, leaving no time to develop future leaders, which is the leader's main responsibility. The hurting will find you. You will have to find the hungry.

You have two choices in your leadership. Do everything yourself or get others to help you carry the load. In Numbers 11:16–17 we read: "Then the LORD said to Moses, 'Gather for me seventy men of the elders of Israel whom you know to be the elders of the people and officers over them, and bring them to the tent of meeting, and let them take their stand there with you. And I will come down and talk with you there. And I will take some of the Spirit that is on you and put it on them, and they shall bear the burden of the people with you, so that you may not bear it yourself alone.'"

This word from God to Moses is thousands of years old, but could be taught at Harvard Business School as well as any Christian leadership conference. It is still relevant and needed. Our willingness and determination to work through others, more than anything else, may well define our effectiveness and success in ministry.

Today is the day of the team and collaborative leadership, not "the Lone Ranger." I have been in the hiring position numerous times through the years, and the person I'm always looking for is the one who does ministry *through* people, not for people or with people. Delegate or suffocate, which will it be?

From time to time the pastors I coach ask if there are any issues that the leaders I coach share in common. The answer is a resounding yes. There are two:

1. Personal organization and energy stewardship;
2. Selecting the right people and forming teams to work with them.

Most of the leaders I meet with are overwhelmed and over committed because they have taken on too much. More than once I have thought that someone could open a business to help people manage their e-mail! Most of us are on e-mail overload, and it is killing our energy and our productivity for the kingdom. We need, by God's grace, to do a better job of allocating our time and being more efficient in our ministry, which is what God wanted for Moses.

Because of the state of many families today and the many children who are growing up in single parent homes with no dad, more and more of our time will be spent in counseling and creating support groups to care for people in such situations. It is imperative that we raise up other hungry leaders, otherwise the weight of the issues and problems will sink us. Fortunately Brent saw this and dealt with it before it was too late and he became another ministry casualty.

I have thought a lot about the importance of picking the right people. No decision, it seems to me, has more long-range consequences than inviting the right people to be among those closest to me. In my role as a leader developer, I am always observing people as to future potential because I believe that one of the most important jobs of a leader is spotting, recruiting, and developing the next generation of leaders.

In Mark 3:13 we read, "And he went up on the mountain and called to him those whom he desired, and they came to him." Later, Jesus spent a whole night in prayer and then chose who would be his apostles. In Acts 1:24 the need presented itself to select someone to take Judas's place: "And they prayed and said, 'You, Lord, who know the hearts of all, show which one of these two you have chosen.'" The eleven disciples understood two things: (1) Only God knew the hearts of those who were candidates for leadership; and (2) They needed God's help to make a good choice. As we read about Paul in the book of Acts, and as he counsels Timothy and Titus in his letters to them, we see that picking good leaders is always on his mind.

It is becoming increasingly clear to me that the thing that can maximize the ongoing effectiveness and fruitfulness of God's ministry through me, making it a joy and not a headache, is having the right people around me. I need to be extremely prayerful and careful in making these choices. As I coach leaders, one of the issues that surfaces on a weekly basis is the need for God's wisdom in selecting people to be part of the leadership team. There are bad situations in many churches because people have not made good choices regarding key players. Often, the wrong people are on the leadership team, or they are serving in the wrong roles.

I caution leaders against picking key players on the basis of friendship, business success, or popularity, but rather making choices based on the person's innate, God-given ability to do what needs to be done coupled with appropriate people skills so as to be a positive and contributing team member.

I find that many pastors and leaders move much too fast and don't do their homework before inviting leaders into the inner circle. Several pastors I know have been set back for months due to poor choices that caused one problem after another. I find myself telling my coaching clients over and over again to pray, get the counsel of others, take your time, don't be in a hurry, interview people several times, ask good questions, look at their character issues, look at their people skills, and don't get fooled by fancy talkers and winsome personalities.

In *Good to Great,* Jim Collins has some excellent insight when he suggests that we "get the right people on the bus and in the right seats."[2] I have begun to think of building a good leadership team in terms of two stages: (1) Inviting the right people to get on the team bus based on *character and chemistry;* and (2) Getting the right people in the right seats on the team bus based on *competency and capacity.*

Let's explore these two.

1. Inviting the *right people* to get on the team bus with you. I believe there are general characteristics that are foundational regardless of the role a person might play on the team. Among these essential character traits are a vital, deep, and growing walk with Jesus; integrity; faithfulness; follow-through; philosophical, mis-

sional, and doctrinal alignment with the organization; and good chemistry with the rest of the team.

2. Getting the people in the *right seats* on the team bus. In his excellent book *First Break All the Rules*, Marcus Buckingham offers this advice: "If you want to turn talent into performance, you have to position each person so that you are paying her to do what she is naturally wired to do. You have to cast her in the right role."[3]

You bring in key people with proven character, track records of faithfulness, and a strong work ethic, and then you place them in roles that fit their God-given talents. You don't place people based on promise or potential but based on proven performance; you should already know what they are gifted to do and have already done.

That is why, if possible, it is always best to "hire from within," so you know what a person can and has done rather than what they tell you they think they can do. The surest way to identify each person's talent is to watch his or her behavior over time. You cannot bring out of a person what God has not built in.

You don't train for talent, you hire for talent. All the training in the world won't change a person's God-given DNA or help him or her be somebody God never intended. A person who doesn't think in detail, and never has, will never have this as a strength and should not be in a role where that is a major expectation. Oh, the issues I have dealt with where the leader cannot understand why so-and-so just doesn't get it or can't learn XYZ! Move people into roles that tap into who God made them. Marcus Buckingham says, "People don't change that much. Don't waste your time trying to put in what was left out. Try to draw out what was left in. That is hard enough."[4]

I encourage you, I implore you, as a leader, to take your time in selecting key people for your leadership inner circle. Look for vibrancy in their walks with Jesus and look for hard-working people of strong character. Once you select them to join you, take the time to make sure what you ask them to do fits who God made them to be. Then sit back and enjoy watching God work through them.

Jesus, forgive me for spending so much time with the hurting and thereby overlooking the hungry leaders that could help lead. Forgive me for what I have done to my family and our relationship by doing too much alone and by myself. By your grace, rebirth a vision of what our ministry could look like with more capable leaders on board, and give me the personal discipline to spend more time with potential leaders.

FOOD FOR THOUGHT

1. Write down the names of one to three potential leaders you will prayerfully consider for leadership.
2. Starting with Exodus 18:21, develop some criteria you will use in selecting those you will invest in.
3. If you are currently doing too much, list several activities you will begin that can help replenish you.

9

ALLOWING INFORMATION TO REPLACE TRANSFORMATION

It's not what you know, but what you do,
in dependence on the Holy Spirit, with what
you know that makes the difference.

It's time for a short review of all the leaders we have met at CCC and what we have learned from them.

THE STORY

Norm, the lead pastor, replaced Jesus with ministry. The ministry had become Norm's mistress, his functional savior. He looked to ministry results for his significance, joy, and satisfaction, instead of looking to Jesus. We will revisit Norm in the next chapter to see how he ended up.

Jim, the executive pastor, replaced contentment with comparison, but was convicted by the Holy Spirit to confess and repent to his family and the church staff. He became a huge help with other staff members.

Jason, the good-looking pied piper, replaced humility with pride. Many of the staff tried to help him see what he was becoming, but he would not listen. He eventually left CCC, and ultimately disqualified himself for ministry.

Chris fell early into the trap of replacing pleasing God with pleasing people. The Lord did a deep work of grace in Chris, and he had a great time at CCC overseeing youth. He eventually moved on to plant a church.

Suzie, children and women's ministry director, replaced vision with busyness and was either unable or unwilling to become the visionary leader the church needed to oversee the women and children's ministries. She was released from her role. It was the hardest decision Jim ever had to make. The decision was tough on her, and she and her family soon started to attend another church in the area.

Bob, elder over finances, had replaced fearless faith with financial frugality. He held the visionary staff as hostages, and loved doing it. With grateful hearts, they watched Bob leave on his own and move to be closer to his kids.

Worship director Bryan replaced dealing with difficult conflict with artificial harmony. He was not able to stand up for his convictions and make the tough calls when needed. It got to the point where Bryan no longer enjoyed his role or felt he should continue. He and Jim agreed that he should step down. Bryan remained at CCC helping where he could, but he was no longer in a leadership role.

Brent, pastor of counseling/support groups, replaced ministering to potential hungry leaders with focusing on perennially hurting people. He exhausted himself and his wife, Patty, by not spending some time developing other leaders. God opened his eyes from Exodus 18, and they both turned the corner and had a much healthier counseling and support group ministry as a result—with great teams working under them.

PRINCIPLE AND PRACTICE

Now let's spend some time addressing the mistake the members and regular attenders at CCC made by overemphasizing numbers. Because of Norm's penchant for wanting to grow the church quickly and numerically, people paid less attention to quality than quantity. Norm was concerned that people attending CCC understood the basics of the Christian life, but he was not equally concerned with the degree of their spiritual transformation. This is often true of larger churches that focus on big events and attendance.

When Norm tried to ascertain what was happening with the church, he focused on how many were in this group or that group—how many in the youth group, children's ministry, small groups, at special events, etc. Because quantity was a higher value than quality, people at CCC gradually made the mistake of replacing transformation (quality) with information (quantity). They were a Bible-teaching church. But they were at their core becoming a transactional (lots of activities) but not transformational (life change) body of believers.

They got lots done and filled up many rooms, but real life transformation was becoming an endangered species, a rare sighting at CCC. The staff believed that this change was happening because most of them were working long hours and trying to produce the results Norm was expecting and demanding. The numbers were growing and Norm was delighted.

This change can often happen to theologically correct and doctrinally precise Bible-teaching churches. It can begin in Sunday school classes where progress is measured by how many right answers children give and by how well they know the Bible stories and characters. Later, a rite of passage is a celebration when teenagers can recite the various catechisms and the lists of names and events they have committed to memory over years of Sundays. Far less attention is given to a living and vital relationship with Jesus and the fruit of a life that has been changed by him.

CCC was experiencing the "always learning and never able to arrive at a knowledge [experience] of the truth" that Paul speaks of in 2 Timothy 3:7. It is eighteen inches from your head to your heart, but it is the longest eighteen inches in the world. The thing that makes the Christian church a veritable reality to the non-Christian world is the disciples who have been, and continue to be, transformed by the living Word of God through the Holy Spirit (Heb. 4:12).

Over my years in ministry, I have been a part of churches who equated information with transformation. It just ain't so. Often certain older Christians in a church are admired and respected because they know the Bible well. I don't believe this kind of knowledge alone will catch the attention of a nonbelieving world. It certainly was not what Jesus had in mind when he prayed for us in John 17.

In John 13:17, after Jesus washed the disciples' feet he said, "If you know these things, blessed are you if you do them." Blessing, joy, and spiritual transformation in the Christian life come not as a result of what we know, but what we do with what we know—empowered by Christ, led by him, and done to honor him. Churches need to powerfully proclaim the gospel as well as challenge Christians to embrace, respond to, and obey what they know, not just continue to gather more information, which can result in full heads and empty hearts. We must hear, believe, and respond to the truth being taught. This doesn't happen automatically. That is why I believe Jesus told us to teach people to obey (Matt. 28:20).

A number of years ago I was invited to speak at a church banquet. The host told me that during the meal they would have the first speaker. After the meal attendees would watch a short but challenging film. Then after the film they wanted me to speak to the audience. I thought, "They will have already heard one speaker and received information. They will have watched a film and received more information. Why not move from information to some meditative dialogue that could lead to healthy application resulting in

God-pleasing transformation over time?" The host agreed, and so it went. What he thought of as being novel was part of the way I was thinking at the time, and continue to think. We have too many talking heads and not enough thinking brains and responding hearts.

I was on staff with the Navigators for thirty-eight years. The Navigators have been known as an organization that emphasizes the spiritual disciplines, not for the sake of discipline but for spiritual transformation. We often heard the story about a guy living in upstate New York who allegedly had memorized thousands of verses of Scripture. As the story went, he was in a conversation with Dawson Troutman, the founder of the Navigators, who had become a Christian due to memorized verses that the Holy Spirit used in his conversion. Dawson asked this young man how many verses he knew, and after the response replied that he wished there was one of them working in his life.

This is it. It's not how much you know, but how God is transforming you and taking what you know to develop you into a person who images Jesus as you cooperate with the Holy Spirit.

Replacing transformation with information is a mistake that some leaders make, and it filters down to the people in the pews. Maturity is erroneously equated with how much you know, how many Sunday school ribbons you have, how faithful you are at church activities, and if you can on any and all occasions be the "Bible Answer Man." People are admired as they spit back the right answers and information. They are wrongly assumed to be godly, mature Christians and sadly find themselves stepping into leadership roles.

Here is a good formula to remember:

Information + meditation + repentance + application=transformation.

Understand that application is my responding in the power of the Holy Spirit to what God is making clear to me.

When I was a young Christian, I was in a strong teaching church. This is what it looked like:

1. Sunday school on Sunday for adults with thirty minutes of teaching.
2. Morning worship service after Sunday school with a thirty-minute sermon.
3. Sunday evening worship service with a thirty-minute sermon.
4. Wednesday night service with a thirty-minute sermon.
5. Saturday morning men's breakfast with a thirty-minute teaching.

I found myself receiving five thirty-minute teaching/sermon segments each week with absolutely no opportunity to discuss or digest anything that would help facilitate gospel transformation in my life. There was no vehicle in the church's programming that promoted dialog or thinking toward practical application of what was being taught.

> Jesus, I confess that I have substituted information for transformation in my life and in the way I approach ministry. I have been content with focusing on the number of people showing up, and I have rejoiced in what they know more than in how they are changed. By your grace help me to emphasize what is happening in the heart as opposed to what is accumulating in the head. I look at the outward appearance, but you look at the heart. Help me to see people as you see them.

FOOD FOR THOUGHT

1. Take an honest look at your own holy habits/spiritual disciplines. Are they information or transformation based?
2. When you measure things at your church, is the emphasis only on quantity, or are you looking at the quality of the people who attend?
3. How are you defining spiritual maturity at your church? What needs to change in the way you evaluate how you are doing at making disciples?

10

ALLOWING CONTROL TO REPLACE TRUST

When trust is missing, it is the beginning
of the end of any relationship.

Norm got us rolling in our story about Covenant Community Church. Like many strong and gifted leaders, he started out well but made several wrong turns along the way toward his vision. His first mistake was letting the ministry itself become the motivation for what was done. The gospel and love for Jesus had almost become an afterthought. Others on the staff saw this early on, but Norm didn't see it the same way. We discussed this in detail in chapter 1, so I won't repeat it here, except to say that this initial mistake gave birth to the other ensuing mistakes.

Comparing, pleasing people, avoiding conflict, not spending time with the hungry leaders, busyness, and frugality all stemmed from not keeping Jesus central in all that was being done at CCC and its becoming a superficial church that emphasized information rather than transformation. CCC had become a church that was obsessed with numbers and growth while overlooking the heart. And things only got worse.

THE STORY

Norm became a commandeering control freak to get what he wanted—and to get it faster. What were once suggestions became demands. Norm took away staff member's freedom to make decisions for their own areas of ministry and began making all the decisions himself. CCC had become a top-down dictatorial organization that was increasingly robbing the team of the joy and excitement they once had for ministry. They, by edict, had become people pleasers, but the people (in this case) was in essence one person—Lead Pastor Norm.

Trust is the cornerstone of relationships. When a husband or wife doesn't trust his or her spouse or when supervisors don't trust their staff, relationships start to unravel. No attribute is more critical than trust in relationships and none is as rare. Perhaps the worst thing that one person can say to another is, "I don't trust you." There was not only an absence of trust at CCC, but a presence of fear before most meetings as the staff awaited the next command from their General Patton. Norm's main goal was to increase the numbers and ensure that they were one of the fastest growing churches in the area. Several of the staff had sent their resumes out and others talked among themselves about what could be done. Many had made praying for Norm's humility and love for Jesus a key part of their prayers for CCC. Some started to lose hope and envision the worst: a major exodus of staff people and a rapid decline in attendance and giving.

Norm continued to be a solid Bible teacher with an emphasis on what people needed to know. He did not, however, emphasize application and personal transformation. He fell into the belief that if people knew the right stuff (which was his responsibility to deliver), everything would be just fine and God would be pleased. He always had interesting and new insights to share with the people who were hungry for new thoughts, information, and never-heard-of-before tidbits. Many almost worshiped Norm and his gifts. What most didn't know was that he was living a triple life. What he was on Sunday morning was not what he had become with the staff and with his family.

Some of the more mature elders at CCC began talking among themselves as to what might be done to remove Norm. His home life was in disarray and he was not taking care of himself. He seemed both angry and exhausted most of the time. They had talked (off the record) with Pastor Jim and had become aware of the deep concerns some of the other staff members had as well.

For the most part, Norm kept entirely too busy to spend any significant time reflecting on his life and ministry. He considered it wasted "navel-gazing time." Perhaps he was afraid to face the reality of what was happening in his heart, his family, and the church. From time to time he would attend some national conference to stay connected with the movers and shakers around the country and to showcase CCC. But he rarely attended anything that caused him to reflect on personal, family, or ministry issues.

When things were at their worst, and many of the leaders feared the worse, the Holy Spirit stepped in to save his church. Out of the blue on a Friday afternoon Norm received a phone call from a pastor friend in Oregon. A select handful of lead pastors of churches of one thousand or more from the West Coast were meeting at a retreat center in Colorado for four days. Jim saw the list of invitees and decided to go. It never occurred to him to ask the purpose of the retreat or what the agenda might be. It's a good thing he didn't, or he might not have attended.

This retreat, in looking back, was the most important thing that ever happened to CCC in its entire history.

When Norm showed up and looked around for the program, he realized there wasn't any. There wasn't even a guest speaker. The fifteen men who attended spent four days sharing their lives, their sin, their mistakes, their repentance, and their love for Jesus. Norm wasn't prepared for this. He had gone to the retreat to network and showcase CCC and was not expecting the triune God to show up in all his splendor and glory. He had never heard pastors of large, "successful" churches spill their guts like this. For the first day and a half, Norm was like the proverbial deer in the headlights. He saw passing before his eyes his life, his wife and kids, and his ministry, but most of all he saw the filth of his idolatry in vivid colors. He was not the only pastor there who had the surprise of his life. God showed up big time!

Norm was a crushed and broken man. The weeping began and then opened like a floodgate. He finally saw what his staff had been telling him for several years. It became clear what an awful pastor and leader for his staff he had become.

He spent much of the time at the retreat taking long walks, confessing, crying, and making numerous calls to his wife and staff, apologizing and confessing his sin. He could hardly wait to get home and begin to make things right.

He had several heartfelt talks in Colorado with some old friends he hadn't seen in years. What an eye-opening, heart-opening, soul-opening four days the Lord had orchestrated for his servant Norm, as well as the other fourteen men.

When he returned home, he set up a staff/elder retreat to revisit and rethink everything at CCC. He wanted them to be open and he asked for honest input, which was something he hadn't asked for in months, maybe years. What an answer to the prayers of staff and elders! They could hardly believe their eyes and ears.

Norm told his staff that before going to the retreat, he had been on the verge of a breakdown. He had been angry and in poor health, and he had considered leaving the ministry and possibly even his marriage. His wife, too, had considered a divorce, but had not mentioned it to Norm. As bad as it had looked from the ministry perspective, it had been even worse for Norm on a personal and family level.

After the staff/elder retreat, the first change they implemented was turning much of the day-to-day decision making over to Pastor Jim and a few key elders. Norm took six months off for some serious marriage counseling, physical rest, personal introspection, and renewal in his walk with Jesus.

Before leaving for his sabbatical, Norm shared everything with the congregation, to the shock and applause of the church family. Both he and his wife wept openly and unashamedly. Through the repentance of their lead pastor, CCC had begun the journey back to its first love (Rev. 2:4–5). Jim and the team did an admirable job of leading in Norm's absence, and upon his return they found that they had a new pastor and a new church. God is good! It took several years for CCC to heal from numerous serious mistakes, but they were on the road to renewal.

PRINCIPLE AND PRACTICE

Looking back over forty-three years of ministry, I would say that I have worked for more controlling leaders than trusting leaders. Anger is the key emotion I have seen come from controlling leaders. First Peter 5:3 reminds leaders not to be "domineering." The NIV translates it as "lording it over," and the King James has it as "being lords." All of these translations point to being a controlling leader.

At the heart of a controlling leader might be insecurity and fear.

- Fear that someone might outshine me;
- Fear that something might go wrong;
- Fear that someone's failure might tarnish my reputation;
- Fear that others might not do things as perfectly as I would do them.

In *Leaders Who Last*, I write about four key responsibilities of a leader. We are to shepherd, develop, equip, and *empower*.

Empowering people has to do with creating an atmosphere that frees people to be their best and do their best for the Savior. Among other things, it means not controlling things too tightly and giving people more freedom to innovate/create and put some of their own ideas and personality into their work.

It means not falling into the "command and control" style of leadership, which was so prevalent in yesteryear but is thankfully on the way out. To empower people means learning how to lead people without controlling them. Proverbs 16:15 says, "In the light of a king's face there is life, and his favor is like the clouds that bring the spring rain." The Message paraphrases this verse as, "Good-tempered leaders invigorate lives; they're like spring rain and sunshine." I like that. Good leaders invigorate the lives of people they lead. One way to do this is to not overcontrol the way people do their work. Holding people responsible for reasonable results and controlling them is not the same.

Here are seven warning signs from Pastor Ron Edmondson that you may be a controlling leader:[1]

1. People start apologizing prior to approaching you with a new idea.
2. You don't really know how people feel about you, but you assume they all approve of your leadership.
3. You assume you are always right.
4. You enjoy keeping others with less information than you have.
5. You think you should be involved in making all the decisions.
6. You fear others being in control of a project.
7. You are the final word on every decision.

If a leader:

- leads through control instead of collaboration;
- always has to be right and seldom or never admits to being wrong;
- uses anger as his primary means of getting results;
- does most of the talking and very little of the listening;
- always has to have all the answers and provide all the solutions;
- always gets what he wants regardless of the price others pay;

- feels threatened by those who are better at something than he is;
- has to have an opinion on every subject and issue;

then biblically, he isn't a true leader!

People like this might have the biggest offices. They might have the fanciest titles on their business cards. They might have the greatest power. They might make the most money. They might be in the marketplace or in the church. They might hold the top position of boss, supervisor, or manager. But they are not the kind of leaders Jesus is looking for: "The greatest among you shall be your servant. Whoever exalts himself will be humbled, and whoever humbles himself will be exalted" (Matt. 23:11–12).

Let me close this chapter with some practical ideas adapted from *Bits & Pieces* on moving from being controlling to being empowering.

The more freedom you give people to do their jobs the way they'd like to do them, the more satisfaction they'll get from their work.

Most leaders are supposed to be a little smarter than other people and, in most respects, they probably are. But if leaders insist on doing all the thinking for their organizations, if everything has to be done *their* way, what's left for the people who work for them to be proud of?

How much personal satisfaction can there be in doing a job that is completely programmed, where your muscles or brain are used to perform repetitive operations already planned and dictated by someone else?

There ought to be something in every job that's satisfying to the person who does it. Unfulfilled people can be just as serious a problem as inefficient methods.

Creating a climate that gives people some independence, without losing control, takes a lot of leadership skill. Here are some techniques that are used by many successful leaders:

- Manage by objectives. Give especially capable people a clear idea of the results you want to achieve and leave the methods to them.
- Suggest methods rather than dictate them, with the understanding that people are free to devise something better.
- Consult people affected by a problem or a proposed change and ask them for their ideas, regardless of whether you think you need them.
- Enrich jobs by delegating decisions as far down the line as possible. If a worker is capable of being trained to make a certain decision intelligently, why have it referred to a supervisor? If a supervisor is capable, why refer to someone above?
- Guide your people to think of constructive suggestions you may already have in mind rather than simply present them yourself.
- Eliminate needless rules and allow people as much freedom and mobility as possible, as long as they produce excellent results and don't interfere with others.

Leaders who successfully practice these things will enjoy excellent morale among their people. If people can lead in this way without abdicating responsibility—without losing total control—they'll also get excellent results.

Jesus, it is clear to me that I spend more time controlling rather than trusting. I tend to micromanage people in my world rather than trusting you through them. I confess it as sin. I repent and accept your forgiveness and graciously ask for your help to experience change in this area of my life.

FOOD FOR THOUGHT

1. Why do we find it so easy to control and so hard to trust God and others?
2. What has Jesus made clear to you from this chapter on how to trust more?
3. Do you have a controller on your team? With God's grace, what can you do to help him or her see the sin in this and repent?

AFTERWORD

Upon finishing this book, I remembered a pastor who had a very difficult decision to make. He had invested a considerable amount of time pastoring a staff person through some behavioral and performance issues. He had bent over backwards to try to keep him on the team—he tried to help him see the mistakes.

After doing everything he could possibly think of, the pastor realized that things were just not going to improve. With a heavy heart, he let him go. Situations such as this are always heartbreaking, and they keep good shepherds up at night. Letting people go is the last resort. You do everything you can from the first interview to ensure a good fit, a good ministry, and longevity, but sometimes when things do not work out, the tough decision has to be made. But if at all possible, you want to pastor a person through the issue in such a way that helps him see and understand the problem, repent, and experience the power of the gospel in his situation.

Sometimes the problem is a result of a hiring mistake, and is thereby a leadership mistake. The front-end process was not thorough enough. In a Twitter post on April 17, 2010, Rick Warren wrote, "Hire slowly and fire quickly." Although it sounds harsh, there is wisdom here. If we hire slowly (and thoroughly), we won't have to fire as much. However, even when we do interview and hire well, things can happen down the road that cause a person to no longer fit with the ministry. In either case, the person needs to be let go quickly, as this will be the best for the person, the team, and the ministry.

If you have a Norm, Jim, Jason, Chris, Suzie, Bob, Bryan, or Brent in your midst, the key question is, how can you pastor them through their "mistakes," assuming they are open for this? What can you do, with God's help, to uncover the deeper issues of the heart, the "why" behind the "what" so that the gospel can shine on the situation? Hopefully this will militate against having to let them go.

Paul shares his heart in 2 Corinthians 11:28 when he says, "There is the daily pressure on me of my anxiety for all the churches." I share his anxiety and concern as I look at the church scene today. I grieve over critical and serious mistakes that are being made.

As John Maxwell says, "Everything rises or falls on leadership."[1] My experience bears this out.

Two coworkers of mine once walked out of a church they were visiting on a Sunday morning for the first time. On that particular Sunday, the lead pastor announced his resignation due to a moral failure. As my coworkers discussed the resignation, they agreed with one another that it didn't need to happen and determined to do something about it. Out of that conversation came Ministry Coaching International, an organization I have worked with for six years.

It didn't need to happen!

Many of the mistakes leaders make don't need to happen either, but they do, and the frequency with which they happen is cause for alarm. Covenant Christian Church with its series of mistakes might not look much different from the church you currently are in, and that should give you cause for alarm. As a result of serious leadership mistakes, bad things happen. As go the leaders, so goes the church.

Many people who study the state of churches in the United States find that most are either plateaued or dying. Some of the reasons for this dismal picture can be found in the mistakes profiled in this book. Serious mistakes can result in:

- Leaders leaving organizations on their own;
- Leaders being asked to leave;
- Leaders going to jail;
- Leaders' marriages or families falling apart;
- Leaders splitting churches;
- Leaders causing many people to become cynical about church;
- Leaders causing the unbelieving community to laugh in derision;
- Churches selling their property;
- Shame and disgrace being brought to the name of Jesus.

In the life of CCC we have explored the following critical mistakes:

1. Allowing ministry to replace Jesus
2. Allowing comparing to replace contentment
3. Allowing pride to replace humility
4. Allow pleasing people to replace pleasing God
5. Allowing busyness to replace visioning
6. Allowing frugality to replace fearless faith
7. Allowing artificial harmony to replace difficult conflict
8. Allowing perennially hurting people to replace potential hungry leaders
9. Allowing information to replace transformation
10. Allowing control to replace trust

When preparing to write this book, I compiled a secondary list of mistakes that could be addressed:

- Allowing selfish ambition to replace godly ambition
- Allowing reactive to replace proactive
- Allowing discouragement to replace dreaming
- Allowing teaching to replace training
- Allowing tactical to replace strategic
- Allowing politics to replace principles
- Allowing talking to replace listening
- Allowing careless firing to replace careful hiring
- Allow competence to replace character
- Allowing pornography to replace purity

If I don't live long enough to write *Mistakes* part 2, at least you know what else you should be aware of in your church, ministry, family, or business.

As I reflect on all of the mistakes listed above, and as I think back on my own experiences with the fifteen churches I have personally been a part of in my forty-three years of ministry, I want to share these closing thoughts:

1. The more that leaders have their identity and worth in Jesus—who he is and what he did through his cross and resurrection—the less chance there will be to fall into any fatal mistakes.

2. I pray over 1 Chronicles 4:10 most every day for anointing, opportunities, and protection. I ask for protection from lust by praying for purity; pride by praying for humility; greed by praying for contentment; and anger by praying for patience. If I fall into big trouble, it will probably be in one of these four areas. Praying daily over them and being aware of the warning in 1 Peter 5:8 that the Devil is patiently waiting to devour keeps me alert and watchful in the Spirit. It is noteworthy that verse 8 is in the middle of Peter's words to leaders. The Evil One is especially after leaders and will use their mistakes to inflict great damage.

3. We need to ask for wisdom and boldness to recognize these mistakes and to take action when God makes it clear to us.

4. As you have journeyed with me in the life of Covenant Community Church and some of its leaders' serious mistakes, I trust you have heard the Holy Spirit speaking to your heart. Here are some things to think about as you apply this book to your life and ministry:

- You may have seen one of these mistakes coming and helped your church avoid it. Thank you, Jesus!
- You may be in the middle of one of these critical mistakes and now have some wisdom and courage from Jesus on what he would want you to do.
- You may be in a church where the mistakes have been going on for years and are obvious to everyone, but no one is willing

to deal with them. God will give you the courage to speak out, rather than put your head in the sand like others have been doing.

- Your church may be experiencing the shockwaves of one or more of these mistakes, and the story of CCC may give you hope that the Lord can yet redeem those mistakes and bring good out of them.

This is meant to be a book of hope, not despair. The triune God is bigger than our mistakes and will work his plan and purpose in spite of them. They don't have to have a tragic end. They can have a triumphal end! Covenant Christian Church has their best days ahead of them and so does your leadership situation, by God's grace!

NOTES

Chapter 1: Allowing Ministry to Replace Jesus
1. Henri Nouwen, quoted in Dallas Willard, Dave Ferguson, and others, "Where I Find Refreshment," in *Leadership Journal* (November 21, 2011): np.
2. "Come Thou Fount of Every Blessing," Robert Robinson, 1758.

Chapter 2: Allowing Comparing to Replace Contentment
1. Robert Fulghum, *All I Ever Needed to Know I Learned in Kindergarten* (New York: Ballantine, 2003), 124.
2. John L. Mason, *An Enemy Called Average* (Tulsa, OK: Honor Books, 1990), 20.

Chapter 3: Allowing Pride to Replace Humility
1. François Fénelon, quoted in Gary L. Thomas, *Thirsting for God: Spiritual Refreshment for the Sacred Journey* (Eugene, OR: Harvest House, 1999), 132.
2. Ibid., 135.
3. C. J. Mahaney, *Humility: True Greatness* (Sisters, OR: Multnomah, 2005), 22.

Chapter 4: Allowing Pleasing People to Replace Pleasing God
1. Ira Chaleff, *The Courageous Follower: Standing Up to and for Our Leaders* (San Francisco: Berrett-Koehler, 2003).
2. Ibid., 12.

Chapter 5: Allowing Busyness to Replace Visioning
1. Marcus Buckingham, *The One Thing You Need to Know: About Great Managing, Great Leading, and Sustained Individual Success* (New York: Free Press, 2005), 59–63.

Chapter 7: Allowing Artificial Harmony to Replace Difficult Conflict
1. Bill Hybels, sermon, "Tough Love," November 17, 1985, Willow Creek Community Church.

Chapter 8: Allowing Perennially Hurting People to Replace Potential Hungry Leaders

1. Gordon MacDonald, *Restoring Your Spiritual Passion* (Nashville: Oliver-Nelson, 1986), 88, quoted in Dave Kraft, *Leaders Who Last* (Wheaton, IL: Crossway, 2010), 131.

2. Jim Collins, *Good to Great: Why Some Companies Make the Leap and Others Don't* (New York: Harper Business, 2001), 13.

3. Marcus Buckingham, *First Break All the Rules: What the World's Greatest Managers Do Differently* (New York: Simon & Schuster, 1999), 148.

4. Ibid., 57.

Chapter 10: Allowing Control to Replace Trust

1. Ron Edmondson, "7 Warning Signs You May Be a Controlling Leader," Jan. 10, 2011, www.ronedmondson.com.

Afterword

1. John Maxwell, *John Maxwell on Leadership* (blog), Nov. 28, 2011, http://johnmaxwellonleadership.com/.

 RE:LIT

Resurgence Literature (Re:Lit) is a ministry of
the Resurgence. At theResurgence.com you will
find free theological resources in blog, audio,
video, and print forms, along with information
on forthcoming conferences, to help Christians
contend for and contextualize Jesus's gospel.
At ReLit.org you will also find the full lineup of
Resurgence books for sale. The elders of Mars
Hill Church have generously agreed to support
Resurgence and the Acts 29 Church Planting
Network in an effort to serve the entire church.

FOR MORE RESOURCES

Re:Lit – relit.org
Resurgence – theResurgence.com
Re:Train – retrain.org
Mars Hill Church – marshill.org
Acts 29 – acts29network.org

CHALLENGING LEADERS TO A NEW WAY TO LIVE, LEAD, AND MAKE A LASTING DIFFERENCE IN THE LIVES OF OTHERS

ONLY 30% OF LEADERS LAST
see page 20 for more

The Christian life is like a race, and too many Christian leaders stumble, burn out, or veer off track. What will it take for you to be a leader who finishes well? This book models a practical and godly approach to leadership that will equip pastors, elders, and small group and volunteer leaders. Part of the Re:Lit series.